For years Charles L. Allen has been loved and respected by the thousands who have heard him preach. He knows the pain and loneliness of living by himself and has written this book from the depths of his own experience. You Are Never Alone will help all those who are alone in this world to escape the rut of self-pity, gloom, fear, and sadness that solitude can bring. Examining the many kinds of loneliness he has encountered in his ministry, Dr. Allen shows you how to find the strength and understanding you need to take the loneliness out of living alone. This beloved author shares poetry, prose, and faith-building anecdotes that will assure you of God's continual presence and intervention in times of despair. You'll learn to trust Him to produce joy from your sorrow, turn disappointment into opportunity, and change failure into victory.

BY Charles L. Allen

Charles L. Allen

You Are Never Alone

Power Books

Fleming H. Revell Company
Old Tappan, New Jersey

Library of Congress Cataloging in Publication Data

Allen, Charles Livingston, date.
    You are never alone.

    1. Loneliness.   2.   Christian life—Methodist authors.   I.   Title.
BV4911.A57   248'.48'76   78-374
ISBN 0-8007-5145-0

This is for my wife, Leila,
With my unceasing prayers that she come home.

CONTENTS

7

PREFACE

The reason for *You Are Never Alone* is very personal for me. Two and a half years ago, my wife's heart stopped beating. The ambulance came and the men got her breathing again. For two weeks she was on a special machine to help her breathe. Then gradually she began to breathe on her own. During these two and a half years I have prayed for her, as Saint Paul says, "without ceasing." People all over the world have been praying for her. For more than a year I "hoped" she would recover. Gradually, her responses have increased to the point that I now "believe" she will recover.

During these years, I have learned something about living *alone*. I have experienced for myself what many hundreds have told me about their experiences. In the church where I am pastor we have an average of four funerals a week. I see couples separated by *death*. I counsel with many couples who are experiencing *divorce*. (Sometimes divorce is more of a burden to bear than is death.) Then there are numbers of young people who have not had the opportunity to marry. They know the meaning of *disappointment*. Of course, some live alone because they *decide* to do so.

These Four *D*s are only part of the picture. I have sought to deal with the issues that people who are living alone have revealed to me. Often I will get fifty letters in a week from people who are alone. As pastor of a church with more than eleven thousand members, I have come personally to know a large number who are *alone*.

This is not a "mournful" book, however. I have tried to identify with the problems we "aloners" face, but I have given more space to the answers—and there *are* answers. Living alone is not all bad—and even the bad can be faced and dealt with.

Before Leila got sick, I would not have written this book. I could not have written it. Now I share it with others who are alone, in the spirit of the words of John Fawcett's hymn:

> We share each other's woes,
> Our mutual burdens bear . . . .

Also, however, we share each other's faith and triumphs. *Living alone* does not mean we are defeated, because *We Are Never Alone*. This book is about many other factors in addition to the Four *D's* I mentioned before. The end of the book is *believing our future in*. That we can do! And we can thank God we can win through the victories.

Living alone is not the same as being lonely. Much of this book is written to help those of us who are alone—*not* to be lonely. May everyone who reads these pages find the strength and understanding that leads to happy living.

I express appreciation to my fellow minister, Dr. D. Orval Strong, for reading the manuscript and making valuable suggestions; to Mrs. Constance Ward and Mrs. Judy Saenz for typing the manuscript; and to Dr. Clarence J. Forsberg for permission to use certain material from his sermons.

CHARLES L. ALLEN
First United Methodist Church
1320 Main Street
Houston, Texas 77002

You Are Never Alone

1

No One Else
Can Be Born for You

Joyce Kilmer, who wrote the beautiful poem which begins, "I think that I shall never see, A poem lovely as a tree . . ." wrote another poem which is not as well known and not nearly so inspiring. In fact, there is tragedy even in the title, which is "The House With Nobody in It." It really is not a great poem yet many people will find deep meaning in it as they read:

Whenever I walk to Suffern, along the Erie track
I go by a poor old farmhouse with its shingles broken and black.
I suppose I've passed it a hundred times
But I always stop for a minute
And look at that house, the tragic house,
The house with nobody in it.

I've never seen a haunted house,
But I hear there are such things;
That they hold the talk of spirits,
Their mirth and sorrowings.
I know this house isn't haunted,
But I wish it were, I do;
For it wouldn't be so lonely
If it had a spirit or two.

If I had a lot of money
And all my debts were paid,
I'd put a gang of men to work,
With brush and saw and spade.
I'd buy that place
And I'd fix it up the way it used to be
And I'd find some people who wanted a home
And I'd give it to them, free.

So whenever I go to Suffern,
Along the Erie track,
I never go by that empty house
Without stopping and looking back.
It hurts me to look at the crumbling roof
And the shutters falling apart,
For I can't help thinking the poor old house
Is a house with a broken heart.

There is tragedy in emptiness and many people who are living alone feel it. Being by yourself oftentimes is like living in a house with nobody in it. This can be a dangerous condition in which to live, because many evils can result from it.

Read with me these words of Jesus:

"When the unclean spirit has gone out of a man, he passes through waterless places seeking rest; and finding none he says, 'I will return to my house from which I came.' And when he comes he finds it swept and put in order. Then he goes and brings seven other spirits more evil than himself, and they enter and dwell there; and the last state of that man becomes worse than the first."

Luke 11:24–26 RSV

We have been told over and over that nature abhors a vacuum. Into a life that is empty, all kinds of spirits may come in—both clean and unclean. There seems to be a persistence about wickedness that goodness does not have. If a plot of earth is left alone, weeds will grow up in it. In order to have good things—flowers or vegetables—they must be planted and cultivated. Living in an empty house can result in an empty person, but not for long. Evil has a way of coming into emptiness.

Each year I give addresses at several commencement occasions. As I see students walk across the platform and receive their diplomas, I know that some will continue to cultivate their minds, but others will stop studying and never grow any more. They come to a place where everything is ready for them to make use of their talents, but they do not do it. Gradually they become empty people.

I have visited several communities where people go to retire after a life of hard work. They soon find time heavy on their hands. Some give themselves to fishing, golf, shuffleboard, or some other activities. Others spend the day sitting on the benches along the sidewalk. Many sit at home and watch television, but as they are cut off from productive work, life gradually becomes empty.

I do not know the source or who said it, but I have a quotation that goes like this, "Every right-minded person ought to will to live, to live fully, to plunge into the stream instead of standing on the bank. A cynic stands on the bank and criticizes swimmers. When a wave comes along and sweeps him off, he feels wronged." As long as a life is empty, there is no chance for love, for dreams, for all of the things that make life worth living. The person who is willing to live with emptiness is taking the risk of having something bad happening. The truth is, emptiness is an impossible situation. Eventually, the house or the life is filled with something. It is a poor old house with nobody in it.

Like a Lonely Bird

In Psalm 102, we read these haunting words; "I am like a vulture of the wilderness, like an owl of the waste places; I lie awake, I am like a lonely bird on the housetop" (verses 6, 7 RSV). Many people feel like "a sparrow alone upon the house top" (verse 7). It is a lonely feeling.

There are many kinds of loneliness. One common loneliness

comes as a result of solitude, that is, being by yourself. One can feel this type of loneliness living in a house alone, out in the forest, or on the prairie. One may feel it in an automobile driving along the highway, or in many other places.

On the other hand, there is loneliness in the crowd. There are those who live in large apartment buildings with people all around them, but they do not feel a part of anyone. Large cities can become very impersonal. One may work in a business with many others and yet feel a very real loneliness.

Suffering can bring loneliness. If you have real pain in your body or in your heart, no other person can experience it with you. Others may sympathize, but in the experience of suffering you are alone.

The loneliness of suffering is also experienced in sorrow. No person can enter into your broken heart and share it with you. Sorrow is a personal and individual, and oftentimes, a very lonely experience.

A feeling of unworthiness can make one very lonely. We remember how the very first people on earth did something they felt was wrong and we read, ". . . and Adam and his wife hid themselves from the presence of the Lord God amongst the trees of the garden" (Genesis 3:8). When one has a feeling of guilt, there is a natural tendency to withdraw, to hide oneself, to be alone.

Many experience what is called *cosmic loneliness.* We are conscious of living in this unlimited universe and we feel lost in the bigness of it all. The psalmist said it this way, "When I look at thy heavens, the work of thy fingers, the moon and the stars which thou hast established; what is man that thou art mindful of him, and the son of man that thou dost care for him?" (Psalm 8:3, 4 RSV). We get lost and overwhelmed in the bigness of it all. Living on a planet with four billion people, in a universe with maybe a billion or ten billion planets, sometimes we feel so little and so insignificant.

There is another type of loneliness. It is the loneliness of judgment. We judge ourselves; society judges us; we are judged by

God. In times of judgment, it's not the crowd that is judged, it is the individual. Sometimes we feel so helpless, so unworthy.

Ever so often, we experience another loneliness. It is at a time of decision. We may seek advice and guidance from many others, but sooner or later, each of us comes to a time when a decision must be made. It is our decision alone. No one else can make it for us and no one else can share in it.

Loneliness can be a very real experience.

Alone May Not Be Lonely

There is a difference in being alone and being lonely. Many people find great happiness and inspiration in moments of aloneness. Loneliness is never happy. Loneliness comes in many different ways. A teenager said to his father, "Dad, I am the loneliest when you do not listen to me and I feel that I cannot get through to you." Many of us experience that loneliness when we feel we cannot communicate with the one we are trying to get through to.

We all need companionship. Even Jesus experienced it. We read, "And he ordained twelve, that they should be with him . . ." (Mark 3:14). Jesus needed people whom He could "get through to." Meaningful human relations are a must for normal people. We can tell ourselves that God loves us. We can have faith and we can pray, but we also need this personal contact.

Recently, a single man was telling me how he went to places where other single people congregate, but that he was finding disappointment in activities with impersonal acquaintances. So-called "fun evenings" were really not much fun for him.

I have found great inspiration in seeing the giant redwood trees in California. I am told that they are the largest living things on earth. Seeing their great size, one would think that the redwood tree is so strong that it is completely independent. Such is not the case. Redwood trees do not have a very deep root system. For this reason, one rarely sees a redwood tree growing alone. Instead, they grow in groves and they intertwine their roots together. In this way these giant trees support one another. So it is

with people. When we become involved with each other, we find
support that we never find alone.

On the other hand, solitude can be a source of strength, if it is
used rightly. Henry Thoreau put it this way, "A man thinking or
working is always alone, let him be where he will." Solitude can
be a very precious experience, if we learn to use it creatively.

Walls Can Be Crumbled

Moss Hart, the Broadway playwright, grew up in a poor family,
in a dingy New York neighborhood. Something happened between him and his father. He did not feel he could ever forgive or
love his father again. Then came Christmas Eve. Later Moss Hart
wrote these words in his autobiography:

. . . On Christmas Eve my father was very silent during the
evening meal. Then he surprised and startled me by turning
to me and saying, "Let's take a walk." He had never
suggested such a thing before, and moreover it was a very
cold winter's night. I was even more surprised when he said
as we left the house, "Let's go down to a Hundred Forty-
ninth Street and Westchester Avenue." My heart leapt
within me. That was the section where all the big stores
were, where at Christmastime open pushcarts full of toys
stood packed end-to-end for blocks at a stretch. On other
Christmas Eves I had often gone there with my aunt, and
from our tour of the carts she had gathered what I wanted
the most. My father had known of this, of course, and I
joyously concluded that this walk could mean only one
thing—he was going to buy me a Christmas present.

On the walk down I was beside myself with delight and an
inner relief. It had been a bad year for me, that year of my
aunt's going, and I wanted a Christmas present terribly—not
a present merely, but a symbol, a token of some sort. I
needed some sign from my father or mother that they knew
what I was going through and cared for me as much as my
aunt and my grandfather did. I am sure they were giving me

what mute signs they could, but I did not see them. The idea that my father had managed a Christmas present for me in spite of everything filled me with a sudden peace and lightness of heart I had not known in months.

We hurried on, our heads bent against the wind, to the cluster of lights ahead that was 149th Street and Westchester Avenue, and those lights seemed to me the brightest lights I had ever seen. Tugging at my father's coat, I started down the line of pushcarts. There were all kinds of things that I wanted, but since nothing had been said by my father about buying a present, I would merely pause before a pushcart to say, with as much control as I could muster, "Look at that chemistry set!" or "There's a stamp album!" or, "Look at the printing press!" Each time my father would pause and ask the pushcart man the price. Then without a word we would move on to the next pushcart. Once or twice he would pick up a toy of some kind and look at it and then at me, as if to suggest this might be something I might like, but I was ten years old and a good deal beyond just a toy; my heart was set on a chemistry set or a printing press. There they were on every pushcart we stopped at, but the price was always the same and soon I looked up and saw we were nearing the end of the line. Only two or three more pushcarts remained. My father looked up, too, and I heard him jingle some coins in his pocket. In a flash I knew it all. He'd gotten together about seventy-five cents to buy me a Christmas present, and he hadn't dared say so in case there was nothing to be had for so small a sum.

As I looked up at him I saw a look of despair and disappointment in his eyes that brought me closer to him than I had ever been in my life. I wanted to throw my arms around him and say, "It doesn't matter . . . I understand . . . this is better than a chemistry set or a printing press . . . I love you." But instead we stood shivering beside each other for a moment—then turned away from the last two pushcarts and started silently back home. I don't know why the words remained choked up within me. I didn't even take his hand on the way home nor did he take mine. We were not on that basis. Nor did I ever tell him how close to him I felt that night—that for a little while the concrete wall between father and son had crumbled away and I knew that we were two lonely people struggling to reach each other.

Act One

One Lonely Woman

I was impressed that the *Houston Post* thought this story was worthy to be printed on the front page of the Sunday edition (July 17, 1977). Reflecting on loneliness, it is a beautiful story. The headline was:

CROSSWORD PUZZLES FILLED BLANKS IN WOMAN'S LONELY LIFE

San Francisco—The woman on the phone was elderly. She called the *Examiner's* sports department, she said, because she was stuck for a word in the crossword puzzle, a four-letter word for a stadium in New York.

She said her name was Ethel.

She was told the word probably was Shea. She said, "Thank you," and hung up.

The next day she called again. This time it was another sports problem in the crossword, a home-run slugger in four letters.

Ruth was suggested. Again she was grateful and hung up. Except this time she said, "Drat it, I ought to have known that myself."

She should have, too. She had been married to Walter "Dutch" Reuther, a great lefthanded pitcher, who had pitched against Ruth and had been on the Yankees with him.

The crossword puzzle became a daily link between the shut-in in her apartment and the sportswriter at his office desk. To him, she was a voice. That's all she was to be. They never met.

Each morning for almost four years, the sportswriter made it his duty to do the puzzle. Each morning she would call to fill in the gaps of her own.

She would let slip little clues as to how she lived. She was alone in the apartment but she had friends down the hall who came to see her. She had a grandson, a fisherman and athlete, "Black Bart" Miller of Hawaii. She was trying to get in touch with him.

One day she said she had to take an ambulance to her doctor's office the next day. It was the only way she could get there.

The next day she phoned to report that the ambulance driver charged her more than $100 for the round trip. A man with her had to pay it out in cash before the driver would take her back. She was going to call District Attorney Joe Freitas about it. And she did.

A few days later, she had a stroke. But she kept on calling: "I'm coming along," she said. "I sound stronger, don't I?"

Each call always got around to the crossword puzzle. Her big day came when the sportswriter couldn't provide a Spanish word and she called the Public Library and got it—and phoned back to straighten out the sportswriter.

Monday and Tuesday she didn't call. Wednesday went by with the finished crossword puzzle still on the sportswriter's desk, unused. Thursday, a man called and asked for the sportswriter.

Ethel Howard Patterson, her maiden name before she married the great lefthanded pitcher, had died, he said, the night before in Saint Francis Hospital.

The sportswriter doesn't know and only suspects that she had been looking for a five-letter word meaning to pass away. And a couple of others meaning lonely and brave.

Two Causes of Loneliness

Loneliness is one of the most influential factors in modern life. One could never list all the causes or the effects of loneliness. From my reading, however, I find that there are two main causes of loneliness which seem to be dominant. One is that the society in which we live is changing at a more rapid pace than ever before. Many people just never catch up and make the adjustment. Second, our society is becoming more and more secular and the idea of a high and holy purpose in life is widely disparaged.

All too quickly people move from a life where they have felt essential and important to a life where they feel superfluous and useless. The loss of responsibility makes one feel unimportant and, in many cases, very lonely.

One is encouraged to develop hobbies and recreational activities, but these do not compensate for the loss of responsible purpose in life. There are many agencies and people working today to develop programs for the aged, but most of these programs are at best only half rewarding.

It is a silly waste of brainpower to have a magic number when one must retire. The consensus today probably is sixty-five years old. Why sixty-five? Why not fifty-five or seventy-five? Let retirement come not by the calendar but by the state of the person.

I have a dear friend who retired when he was forty-four. He had a delightful time until he was forty-seven. Then he went back to his old job and started over again. He is one of the happiest men that I know. I wish it could be that ever so often we could all retire and then start over again when we get ready. But, for most of us, retirement would be the end. Like sticking our finger in a pan of water and withdrawing it, there is no hole left. Once we drop out, there is no place left to go back to.

Loneliness can be a powerful motivator. I am one who believes that out of much of the loneliness in our society today will come some constructive changes in our attitudes toward retiring people and the loss of all that brainpower and experience.

Somebody Cares

The children of Israel were in lonely exile. God commanded His servant Isaiah, "Comfort ye, comfort ye my people . . ." (Isaiah 40:1). God's people were homeless, homesick, and heartsick. They felt that their exile was a judgment of God upon them because of their sins. They felt guilt and despair.

In some way or another, every person experiences lonely exile. You can live in the same house with a person, or several persons, and still feel exiled. Loneliness may come as a result of some specific event—a sudden illness, the loss of a job, the death of a mate, a misunderstanding with a friend, a feeling of dependence when we have nothing to depend on, or in so many other ways. Loneliness can rise in front of us like a brick wall—an empty chair—a hushed silence—an itch but no place to scratch—a feeling of tiredness with no place to lie down—a desire for expression with no ears to hear. One can experience a climate of discomfort but not be able to explain it.

Remember this—it is okay to need to be comforted. It is as blessed to receive comfort as it is to give comfort. It is just as human to need to be consoled as it is to console. We like to identify ourselves with strength, but sometimes we also need to identify ourselves with weakness. Sooner or later, each of us comes to the place of needing to be comforted.

We remember the musical, *Jesus Christ, Superstar.* In it there is a touching scene as Mary Magdalene sings to Jesus:

> Try not to get worried, try not to turn on to
> Problems that upset you oh don't you know
> Everything's alright yes everything's fine
> And we want you to sleep well tonight—
> Let the world turn without you tonight—
> If we try we'll get by so forget all about us tonight—*

Yes, even Jesus had to walk through some lonesome valleys.
To be comforted means to feel that somebody cares.
God is still saying, "Comfort ye, comfort ye my people." For
each of us those words are a promise.

On the other hand, those same words are a command. There
is somebody who needs the comfort that may come through me
or through you. Listen to these words:

> He came singing love.
> He lived singing love.
> He died singing love.
> He ascended in silence.
> If the song is to continue—
> We must do the singing.
>
> AUTHOR UNKNOWN

Happily, we find that in comforting we gain comfort.

The Road to Saint Ives

> Alone, alone, all, all alone;
> Alone on a wide, wide sea!
> So lonely 'twas, that God himself
> Scarce seemed there to be.
>
> SAMUEL TAYLOR COLERIDGE
> *The Rime of the
> Ancient Mariner*

Somewhere I read the riddle:

As I was going to Saint Ives, I met a man with seven wives.
Every wife had seven sacks. Every sack had seven cats.
Every cat had seven kits. Kits, cats, sacks, wives—
How many were going to Saint Ives?

I was never very good at math and trying to make all the
multiplications that riddle calls for, does not inspire me. In fact,

one does not need any math at all to solve that riddle. The answer is *one*. "As I was going to Saint Ives." The rest of the riddle is immaterial; there was only one who was going and I was that one.

For each of us there are times when we are compelled to make a journey alone. Some paths are wide enough for just one person. Some burdens must be carried; some work undertaken; some guilts borne; some decisions made by just one person. There is some "Saint Ives" to which you must journey alone. There are some paths that only you can walk. Some burdens only you can carry. Some guilts that only you can bear. Some decisions that only you can make. No one else can be born for you.

Jesus went alone into the wilderness not once, but again and again. The Bible begins with God alone: "In the beginning God created the heaven and the earth" (Genesis 1:1). The Bible ends with Saint John alone on the Isle of Patmos looking into the life beyond—"And I saw a new heaven and a new earth . . ." (Revelation 21:1).

There is a right kind of aloneness and a wrong kind of aloneness. The right kind is creative: ". . . in quietness and in confidence shall be your strength" (Isaiah 30:15). In aloneness our minds can be most creative. In aloneness we can speak to ourselves most clearly. In aloneness God can speak to us. The wrong kind of aloneness provokes pity, disintegrating of emotions, depreciation of one's self. Loneliness can be a devastating experience.

There are times, though, when you and I must be willing to be separated from those we love. There are times we need to talk to ourselves and say, "What manner of person must I really be?" The one who cannot stand to be alone, should seek to discover why.

EVERYONE'S ALONE

CELIA   No . . . it isn't that I want to be alone,
        But that everyone's alone—or so it seems to me.
        They make noises, and think they are talking to each
            other;
        They make faces, and think they understand each other.
        And I'm sure they don't.

T. S. ELIOT
The Cocktail Party, Act II

MERELY INSULATED

GOMEZ   O, loneliness—
        Everybody knows what that's like,
        Your loneliness—so cozy, warm and padded;
        You're not isolated—merely insulated.
        It's only when you come to see that you have lost your-
            self
        That you are quite alone.

T. S. ELIOT,
The Elder Statesman, Act I

2

It's a Brand-new Ball Game

Thomas Mann, the great novelist and thinker, used to say about any real story, "It always is; it always is; no matter how we may try to say, 'It was!' "

If you listen to a broadcast of a baseball game you may hear the announcer say, "It's a brand-new ball game." That means that the score has been tied. It's like starting all over again.

So it is in life. Many people come to a place where "it's a brand-new ball game." Some situation has developed that has changed the old ball game. We start all over again. When a couple gets married, "It's a brand-new ball game." Also, when they get a divorce, or when one of them dies, or even when they keep living together but stop loving each other. Suddenly—and often without warning—life-changing experiences come. It's a time to begin again. It's something new. In a baseball game, when the score is tied in the fifth inning, they do not go back to the first inning and start over again. They keep on playing. So it is in life; there's a sudden change (or maybe a change not so sudden), but the moment comes for many people when it is *a brand-new ball game*

In a baseball game, at the end of the fourth inning, the score might be five to nothing in favor of one team; then in the very next inning, the other team scores five runs. Now the score is tied and now it is a brand-new ball game. What should be done about it? The team that was ahead and then got tied doesn't sit in the dugout, mourning the fact that they let the other team catch up with them. Instead, they go out on the field and keep on playing.

Another thing: when we find ourselves in a brand-new ball game, instead of counting our losses, there is legitimate reason for a sense of expectancy. The immediate reaction is to be overwhelmed, until we cannot see beyond the gloom. We feel a bit frightened and very uncertain. Then we realize a ball game is still going on, and we are still playing in it. James Whistler and Carl Sandburg both failed as students at West Point. Instead of becoming soldiers, each of these found himself in a brand-new ball game. Whistler became a famous artist, Sandburg a famous writer.

Just because it *is* a brand-new ball game does not mean that you have lost. It does mean that you must keep trying and, thank God, it is a ball game still, even though it's new.

Graduation Time

In these pages I have previously referred to graduation exercises in some school. Year after year, I have given a baccalaureate sermon and then sat back and watched the students file by to receive their diplomas. All these years they have been going to school. That can be a very comfortable and secure situation.

I heard about a very wealthy man who left a stipulation in his will that his son's expenses were to be paid "as long as he was in college." The young man started in college and he just stayed there. When he was sixty years old he had accumulated about a dozen degrees. He never could quite leave and go out into the world on his own!

For these students we see graduating from our colleges and universities each year, it is a time of starting over again. Someone has well said:

> Your life is God's gift to you;
> What you do with it is your gift to God.

Many people come to periods of "graduation." Life has a way of bringing us to the end of one road, and we are forced to start over on some other road.

One of the most remarkable stories in all history is the story of the children of Israel, as they made their way from Egypt, the land of bondage, to the Promised Land. They were led by the brilliant and wonderful Moses. As you read the story in the Book of Exodus, you find that it took them forty years. Actually, if you measured the distance, you will find they could have done it in a matter of days. But God kept them in the wilderness that they might learn the truths of life by that long discipline. Many people have gone through difficult situations before they achieved their highest character—their most winsome personality—their best skills—and their maturity.

When we come to these life-changing moments, why not think of them as times of "graduation." We are graduating from one life to another life. Perhaps we did not want to give up the old life, but we had no choice.

Perhaps no one has said it better than John Oxenham:—

To every man there openeth
A Way, and Ways, and a Way,
And the High Soul climbs the High Way,
And the Low Soul gropes the Low,
And in between, on the misty flats,
The rest drift to and fro.
But to every man there openeth
A High Way and a Low.
And every man decideth
The way his soul shall go.

Let the Wound Heal

In Margaret Mitchell's novel *Gone With the Wind*, old Grandma Fontaine, talking of the bitter experiences of defeat in the war, said:

The whole world can't lick us. But we can lick ourselves by longing for things we haven't got any more and by remembering too much.

Many people suddenly find themselves in a new and frightening situation. They are alone. There is a tendency to look back with regret, remorse, self-reproach, and bitterness. When we do, the result is usually self-defeat. It is natural for radical changes and severe losses to leave us with a feeling of hurt. That wound in our lives need not be permanent, though, if we take several steps. First, we need to recognize that we do have a wound. To ignore or cover up a deep hurt creates more trouble. We catch ourselves reminiscing about the comfortable home in which we used to live, the marriage that was a success, the bank account that was adequate, or a time of health and well-being. As we keep looking back, we keep nursing the wound, and it gets worse and worse and harder to bear. There comes a time when we need to bind up the wound and let it begin to heal.

Surrender or Survival

Is it possible for one to lose the will to survive? Not only is it possible, it happens over and over. Many people feel that oblivion is preferable to existence.

In India there are many miserable human beings sitting on the banks of the sacred Ganges River waiting to die. They have nothing in this life for which to live, and they are looking forward to entering Nirvana. They do not cry out against the social conditions of their country. They do not demand reforms or changes. They merely accept their condition and long for their release.

It is very possible for a person to reach a place where it seems that there is no hope, and no reason to try to build back. They have no heart to start over again. They just look for some release.

On the other hand, there are those who say that no matter what has happened, they still want to live. They do not want to quit now. They are ready to start, to see what is going to happen, to stay a while longer. It's just possible, they reason, that this experience is not the twilight—but the dawn. There are those who are willing to say that come what may, they want to survive. Maybe they are not surviving in the manner that they would like to have survived, but still they want to survive.

Not everything ought to live forever. There are many things that ought to die. There are some things about any one of us that ought to die. On the other hand, every person on this earth has something about himself or herself that is worth saving and that should be preserved. There is something about you that should not be destroyed. When we begin to concentrate on what we have of value, life begins to take on new meaning.

If we really want to survive, we must find other dimensions in life, other reasons for living, other goals for which to strive. We must decide what is important and what is trivial. Surrender or survival—that is the question for many people.

Then—Now—Not Yet

The focus of life can be upon yesterday with its disappointments and rejections, its losses and its hurts—and its misunderstandings and its harshness.

Or, the focus of life can be upon some distant horizon of tomorrow. We decide we are not going to do it today, but tomorrow, or next year. We have a decision to make, but we are waiting until something else happens.

The truth is that the past is a dream that cannot be changed. The future is also a dream that does not even exist. The only real time that we have to live, to be, and to act, is the present. Neither has any birth or any death ever happened yesterday or tomorrow. Birth and death and everything else that is important, happens right now.

I know no other way to tell how strongly I feel about it than to use something very old from the Sanskrit in order to describe the mix of feeling for then, now, and not yet.

> Look to this Day!
> For it is Life, the very Life of life.
> In its brief course lie all the
> Verities and Realities of your existence:
> For Yesterday is but a Dream,

And Tomorrow is only a Vision:
But Today well-lived makes
Every Yesterday a Dream of Happiness,
And every Tomorrow a Vision of Hope.
Look well therefore to this Day!
                                    "Salutation to the Dawn"

The Chinese said, "All the flowers of tomorrow are in the seeds of today." If you can't find God in this day, then you'll not find Him in the past, and I doubt that you'll find Him in the future.

More than any people I know, people who are living alone need the discipline of living *now*—not yesterday and not tomorrow. Living alone, we feel inadequate and many times defeated. As we give ourselves to the present moment, we find new strengths, new powers, and new confidences. It is a marvelous experience when daily living becomes really the end. We are no longer haunted by past unhappiness; we are no longer afraid of future possibilities.

TODAY

There are two days in every week about which we should not worry, two days which should be kept free from fear and apprehension.

One of these days is *Yesterday* with its mistakes and cares, its faults and blunders, its aches and pains. Yesterday has passed forever beyond our control.

All the money in the world cannot bring back Yesterday. We cannot undo a single act we performed. We cannot erase a single word we said. Yesterday is also beyond our immediate control.

Tomorrow's sun will rise, either in splendor or behind a mask of clouds—but it will rise. Until it does, we have no stake in *Tomorrow,* for it is yet unborn.

This leaves only one day—*Today*. Any man can fight the battles of just one day; it is only when you and I add the burdens of those two awful eternities—Yesterday and Tomorrow, that we break down.

It is not the experience of Today that drives men mad; it is remorse or bitterness for something which happened Yesterday and the dread of what Tomorrow may bring.

AUTHOR UNKNOWN

Or, as Annie Johnson Flint has written:

ONE DAY AT A TIME

One day at a time, with its failures and fears,
With its hurts and mistakes, with its weakness and tears,
With its portion of pain and its burden of care;
One day at a time we must meet and must bear.

One day at a time to be patient and strong;
To be calm under trial and sweet under wrong;
Then its toiling shall pass and its sorrow shall cease;
It shall darken and die, and the night shall bring peace.

One day at a time—but the day is so long,
And the heart is not brave, and the soul is not strong,
O Thou pitiful Christ, be Thou near all the way;
Give courage and patience and strength for the day.

Swift cometh His answer, so clear and so sweet:
"Yea, I will be with thee, thy troubles to meet;
I will not forget thee, nor fail thee, nor grieve;
I will not forsake thee; I never will leave."

Not yesterday's load we are called on to bear,
Nor the morrow's uncertain and shadowy care,
Why should we look forward or back with dismay?
Our needs as our mercies, are but for the day.

One day at a time, and the day is His day;
He hath numbered its hours, though they haste or delay.
His grace is sufficient; we walk not alone;
As the day, so the strength that He giveth His own.

The Starting Point

There is a story about a traveler who stopped in a small town. He said to one of the natives: "What is this place noted for?"

The native replied, "Mister, this is the starting point for any place in the world. You can start from here and go anywhere you want to."

That's true of all of us. Wherever we are is the starting place.

"God Shall Prevent Me"

The Fifty-ninth Psalm begins with a prayer of the psalmist asking God to deliver him from his enemies. He speaks of how these enemies rise up against him, how they lie in wait for his soul and how they come in the evening and, he says, ". . . they make a noise like a dog" (verse 6). But then the psalmist says, "The God of my mercy shall prevent me . . ." (verse 10). It is that word *prevent* that we need to underscore. It is an old English word which literally means "go before." The New English Bible translates it that God "shall be my champion." Then the psalmist says, "God shall let me see my desire upon mine enemies" (verse 10). The New English Bible translates it, "I shall gloat over my watchful foes." The point is, we come to these places in life where we are inadequate. Then we have the assurance of the strength of one who is sufficient to meet all of our needs. In the entire journey of life, there are many problems to face. We are constantly changing directions and making new adjustments. We are learning today that many people cannot tolerate smoking. Giving up that habit is not easy. Alcohol is an absolute *no, no* for many, many people. But neither is that an easy enemy to face. There are other enemies from which we pray God to deliver us. If we live long enough, we will retire and there is danger of beginning to feel useless. Growing older is an enemy that many people resent. We face sorrows, temptations, disappointments. There is the matter of our own death. But, then we say with the psalmist, with God's help we need not fear the enemies of life; we can even "gloat" over them. Usually I do not like that word, but in this connection I think it is wonderful. Do not forget, "the God of my mercy shall prevent me." That is, He will be at the crisis when I get there.

George Frederick Handel became half-paralyzed and bankrupt. Life for him had become almost an impossible situation. Yet, in the midst of his worst moment came one of his greatest inspirations. He was inspired to produce an oratorio *The Messiah*. Later he told his friends that when he was composing the "Hallelujah Chorus," he could, as it were, hear angels singing and he wrote the music to which he was listening. Today, when we hear the "Hallelujah Chorus," we cannot remain seated. It would be sacrilegious to hear that chorus without standing. What an inspiration that a half-paralyzed, bankrupt man could write it. Such is the God who goes before us.

John Wesley went to Georgia a missionary. He went home a discouraged failure. Then one night, he went to a prayer meeting and there he felt his heart "strangely warmed." He went out from there to begin preaching. He changed the religious climate of a great nation and started a revival that literally went around the world. In the midst of his failure, God was before him.

Today we have seen tremendous scientific advances. We keep asking ourselves, "What will we do next?" We really need to ask, "What will God do next?" More especially we need to ask "What will God do next in my own life?" We need to remember that we are in the hands of a living God who goes before us and whose power still goes on creating.

I happen to live around the corner from a man who has walked on the moon. None of us knows where we will be walking tomorrow, next week, or next year. There is one thing we can be sure of: God is walking ahead of us.

Let Me Be Aware

A great poetess, Miriam Teichner, wrote the following wonderful words:

> God—let me be aware.
> Let me not stumble blindly down the ways,
> Just getting somehow safely through the days,
> Not even groping for another hand,
> Not even wondering why it all was planned;
> Eyes to the ground unseeking for the light,
> Soul never aching for a wild-winged flight,
> Please, keep me eager just to do my share.
> God—let me be aware.
>
> God—let me be aware.
> Stab my soul fiercely with others' pain,
> Let me walk seeing horror and stain.
> Let my hands, groping, find other hands.
> Give me the heart that divines, understands.
> Give me the courage, wounded, to fight.
> Flood me with knowledge, drench me in light.
> Please—keep me eager just to do my share.
> God—let me be aware.

If you ask yourself the question, "What is awareness?" I believe that one thing you would think about is your possibilities. It is said that we use only a very small fraction of our brain power. That is also true of our physical power. It is also true of our opportunities. Awareness means that we begin to realize something of the infinite potentiality that is within even ourselves. Beyond that, awareness is a deep sensing of other persons. That is, we come to understand that other person. I think Anne Morrow Lindbergh said it best in these words, "Each man is an island, but all men are connected by a common sea. We therefore are aware of the potentiality of the person, but, are not limited by his own limitation."

We go even further in believing that total awareness means a capacity to have fellowship with those who have been released from the limitations of this physical life.

People who live alone have more time to be quiet and to think. We need to set aside moments to make an effort to be aware—to begin to understand in our minds what our ears listen to—to see with understanding what our eyes behold—to begin to respond to the stimulations of life which are all around us—and to get the message from every situation.

"God—let me be aware."

Life's Great Moments

One of the most memorable experiences of my life was one cold, rainy morning just about daylight. I stood on a street corner and watched my oldest son get on a bus and head out for an army camp and a war. I watched that bus until it was out of sight. Never will I ever forget that moment. Many people have experienced similar moments in their own lives. Their plans have been interrupted, and the things they wanted to do had to be put aside. Through no fault of their own, circumstances were such that they had to go into a life that they did not want, that they dreaded, and even feared. It is not an easy time.

It is interesting to make a list of great moments of your life. Such a list could be long. Let me suggest some of the things that come to my mind with the thought that you would think of many other things. I remember when I became a member of the first team in high-school football and I was not a substitute any longer. Going out to start the game was for me a thrilling experience. When I graduated from high school, preached my first sermon, got married, looked into the face of our first baby, accumulated a few extra dollars in a savings account—these were all high moments—and the list could go on.

Then I think of the life of Jesus. Most of the things I have named He never experienced. We do not know very much about His early life. As I have studied the New Testament I have come to feel that His father must have died when Jesus was young.

Being the eldest child in the family, He probably took over His
father's carpenter shop. He did not have a chance to go to
school, or play on the football team. He never got married. He
was not opposed to marriage. I really doubt that He was opposed
to His own marriage. In fact, it is my opinion that He would have
been happy to have been married. The probability is that during
His teens and early twenties, He didn't have time to court. He
probably never had a girl friend. He never became a father, and
of course, He never accumulated any money in the bank.

There are many people who feel cheated in life. When we feel
that way, it's good to make a list of the things that Jesus never
experienced. At about the age of thirty, He felt He could leave
home. Perhaps His younger brothers had taken over the carpenter shop and He felt that they could make the living. Jesus actually started His life when He was thirty years old. That seems late.
There are people today who are thirty years old who feel that life
has passed by them. Yet, as we think of Jesus beginning His work
at the age of thirty, we remind ourselves that we can start at any
age. Whatever your age is, it can be a beginning time.

To begin with, you need to decide to get started. In the second
place, you must believe in what you are planning to do and
believe it is the right thing. Those two factors are essential to
beginning again.

You cannot go back and start over as a baby. You are who you
are, you are the age you are, and you are where you are.

What Color Is Grace?

As I was driving the other day, I turned on the radio and a
group was singing a jukebox version of the great, old hymn
Amazing Grace. I rather enjoyed listening to their souped-up
version of the hymn. I think I heard it as I have not heard it in
many years. I kept thinking of grace and its meaning. For some
strange reason, I wondered what color grace is. That was a new
thought for me. We do use colors to describe our experiences.
We say, "I feel blue." Sometimes when we are angry we "see
red." Somehow, I began to picture grace as green. I thought of

the springtime and how the trees begin to put on new leaves and become green again. Grace to me began to represent new beginnings. Thank God, we can start over again. You have heard it all your life, but read the words of that great old song, as if you had never heard them, and hear those words speaking to you right this moment.

AMAZING GRACE

Amazing grace! how sweet the sound,
That saved a wretch like me!
I once was lost, but now am found,
Was blind, but now I see.

'Twas grace that taught my heart to fear,
And grace my fears relieved;
How precious did that grace appear
The hour I first believed!

Thru many dangers, toils and snares,
I have already come;
'Tis grace hath bro't me safe thus far,
And grace will lead me home.

When we've been there ten thousand years,
Bright shining as the sun,
We've no less days to sing God's praise
Than when we first begun.

JOHN NEWTON

"Another Chance"

One of the dearest friends I ever had and one of the ones I admired the most was Ernest Rogers. He lived in Atlanta, Georgia. For a number of years he was the most popular radio newscaster in that state. Later he wrote a daily column for the *Atlanta Journal*. His column was read by more people than any other feature in the entire newspaper. He went to heaven a few years ago, but he continues to live in the hearts of many, many people.

He graduated from the university and went to work for the newspaper. Later, there came a period in his life when, as he said to me, "I hit bottom." Let it be said to his credit, however, that he did not stay on the bottom. One day he gave me a copy of a poem that he had written. I am not sure that he ever published this poem. I am not sure that many people ever saw it, but I have kept it across the years and I read it with inspiration. Here it is:

> Maybe I failed in the final drive
>   When sinew and nerve and heart
> Had lost the urge and the will to strive—
>   And I played the loser's part . . . .
>
> Those who have drunk from the bitter cup
>   And tasted the dregs of defeat—
> May win again, if lifted up
>   And placed in the mercy seat.
>
> Lord, I search through the darkling skies
>   For a word or a sign or a glance—
> That brings new light to my dimming eyes,
>   From the GOD OF ANOTHER CHANCE.
>
> "Winner take all" is the way of the pack
>   The losers must weep alone;
> The way is hard if they struggle back
>   To try it again on their own.
>
> But there is hope for the winner's share
>   For those who would advance—
> By lifting up abiding prayer
>   To the GOD OF ANOTHER CHANCE.
>
> So down on my trembling knees I fall
>   Though others may look askance—
> To say a prayer to the Lord of All—
>   The GOD OF ANOTHER CHANCE.
>
>   ERNEST ROGERS

3

The One Thing I Want Most
Is to Belong

The pastor of a large church in the center of a big city has a lot of visitors. The other day a young man came into my office. He told me that he had been in prison for three years and now he was starting his life over again. During his conversation he said, "The one thing I want most is to belong."

Nothing runs deeper in human nature than the desire to be accepted, to be appreciated, to be a part of the group. As small children we crave for approval. We try to get attention and recognition. "See how fast I can run," a little boy will say. As a teenager, dreading the possibility of going friendless, one oftentimes will join in crowd behavior really against his own will. As adults, the desire to be a success socially is a driving force. Rarely is there a person who wants to be left out of things.

This desire is really God-given and it is not wrong to possess it. In fact, it is very right to possess it. There is a place for proper self-appreciation and this involves harmonious relations with other people.

Consider the lengths to which some people will go to be accepted. Some will shower praise and attention and gifts on those whose favor they are seeking. Some will make very substantial contributions to some institution in society in order for his or her name to become known and remembered. Universities have been built because of this desire in humanity.

Unfortunately, there are those who will compromise with principle in order to be accepted.

On the other hand, not having a sense of belonging, one can give in to self-depreciation, to despair, and a sense of inferiority. In a world with other people, we need to face the facts about ourselves. We need to consider what we are and what we are not, what we can do and what we cannot do. We do not have to build up our capacities beyond reality. Neither do we have to hide our inadequacies. Really to belong in society one has to be his or her real, true, best self. Be thankful that you are an individual and that you have gifts, whether they be great or small. Realize that there is value in you to your fellow man. Remember that when God made you He made you who you are and He made nobody like you.

Warmhearted recognition is a normal and human desire. All of us need somebody to like us into liking ourselves.

The Pain of Rejection

Recommended reading for the lonely person is the autobiography of Jackie Robinson. It was published several years ago. Even if it is not available in bookstores, it should be in libraries. Reading that book brought back to mind an era which now seems ancient history. Jackie Robinson was the first black man to play baseball in the big leagues. He knew the meaning of rejection as few men who have lived in this country.

Branch Rickey, a really great and wonderful man who spent his life in baseball, was committed to the principle that if a sport were truly national, then no person in the nation should be excluded. He kept looking for the right person to break the so-called color line. Finally, he discovered Jackie Robinson. He explained to him that no matter what happened he had to have control of himself. He was never outwardly to react to any treatment he ever received. He was never to let himself fight back.

Jackie Robinson was coldly ignored by many of his own teammates. Racial slurs were hurled at him, both from the grandstand and from members of the opposing teams. There were obvious attempts to hurt him. There were even phone calls threatening the lives of his children.

One day, however, something happened that changed it all. In his book he describes it this way:

> I had had a miserable start, but I ended the season batting .296 with twelve home runs and eighty-five runs batted in. I led the league in being hit with seven pitched balls (a dubious distinction) and in fielding average for a second baseman with a .983.
>
> The most important thing that happened to me in 1948 as far as I was concerned is that I got thrown out of a game for heckling an umpire. It happened in Pittsburgh. The umpire was Butch Henline. In the fourth inning Henline called a strike on Gene Hermanski. Along with other Dodgers on the bench, I gave Henline what we called the bench jockey treatment, booing and raucously protesting what we felt was a bad decision.
>
> Henline gave us a warning to quit. I continued the heckling. He whirled around, snatched off his mask, and pointed at me. "You! Robinson. Yer out of the game!"
>
> He didn't pick on me because I was black. He was treating me exactly as he would any ball player who got on his nerves. That made me feel great, even though I couldn't play any more that day. One of the newspapers said it *in the best headline I ever got:* JACKIE JUST ANOTHER GUY.

The "pain of rejection" is probably the most prevalent pain on the face of this earth. Also, it is almost the hardest pain to bear. A person can live with pain in the physical body. A person can live with the pain of sorrow, the pain of frustration, or the pain of failure. To be left out of the human race by other humans though is very, very hard to bear. This pain afflicts both the rich as well as the poor, those who live among other people and those who live in isolation, those who are highly honored, and those who feel they have failed in life.

Many of the people that we live with, and work with, and see day by day, are experiencing this "pain of rejection." They are ashamed to let others know how they feel. They use a "don't care" mask to cover the loneliness in their hearts.

When one feels a pain in the body, it is the body's way of saying, "There is something wrong; you need to have it seen about." A toothache sends us to the dentist, a pain in the chest can be very frightening, and the "pain of rejection" can put scars on a life. A little child can be unloved and never really recover from it. A young person can believe that the whole world is against him or her. We see this especially in older people. They have earned the right to enjoy the fruits of their labors, but many times they find those years their very unhappiest, because they feel unwanted and unloved.

There was a time in our society when older people lived with a child in a position of respectful recognition. More and more today the nursing home has become the answer. People can be put in nursing homes and forgotten. Nobody feels any responsibility for them. Their years can be cut much shorter than otherwise.

The "pain of rejection" can be a crippling and life-destroying disease. It can make one bitter and withdrawn. It can drive one to acts of madness, such as assassination, arson, rape, and violence of the very worst sort. Every so often there is a horror story in our newspapers of some mass murder. Study the one who commits it. Almost invariably you find a person with an acute sense of rejection. The truth is that every person has experienced some rejection and there is no need for us to be ashamed of it or to hide it. There is need to give heed to it and deal with it constructively.

First, let us understand that part of the reason that we do not have a feeling of belonging and of being loved is our own fault. In some ways, each of us has invited rejection.

Suppose the question were put to you, "If you could erase anything that you have done during your life, what would it be?" Most of us would have difficulty in answering that question because there are so many things we would like to erase. When asked that question, one person said, "I would erase the critical remarks that I have made of other people." He went on to explain that all too often some critical remark that he made of somebody else had come back to haunt him and to hurt him. Some of our rejection is retaliation for the rejection that we have "dished out."

On the other hand, some of our rejection we have actually wanted and sought. For some strange reason there are people who enjoy being sick. There are others who enjoy being unhappy. There are still others who are ultrasensitive to any action or word that might be interpreted as unfriendly. They actually seem to be happy in feeling that somebody is against them. There are those who enjoy being persecuted.

In the second place, because we are who we are and what we are, there is some rejection that we must expect and accept. Trying to avoid rejection is a self-destructive way to live. There are some right reasons for rejection. You stand for what you stand for, you are the person that you are, you are unwilling to be less than your best. We reject the criminal but also we remember the Crucifixion of the Christ. In every age there are issues to be faced. If you take a stand on an issue, you are certain to face the rejection of those who believe otherwise. It should be that in a democracy we should be willing to insist that others have the same right of decision that we demand for ourselves. Such is not the case. There is something in people who demand rights for themselves, yet reject those who cling to those same rights. To be who you are may result in rejection. If so, so be it.

There is a third point we need to remember about rejection. Having experienced it ourselves, we need to understand it in others. We need to offer ourselves in every way possible to those who need it. In fact, the cure for the "pain of rejection" is the loving of those who are rejected.

In my mail some time ago, came a poem entitled "Little Things." It goes like this:

> It is little things that mean so much
> As we go along through life;

A smile, handclasp, or letter,
    To encourage amidst the strife.
Sometimes a soul discouraged
    Is lifted and given new vim
By another's thoughtfulness
    And kindness unto him.

Sometimes it's true it's just a smile
    That makes one's way more bright;
A soft hand upon your shoulder
    That makes things go more right.
A card, a note, or letter
    Will strengthen and help to lift
Another brother's burden; oh!
    It is not the great big gift!

Sometimes it's just a little thing
    That lifts the heavy load;
A look of understanding
    As we travel life's hard road;
Again it is a little thing
    That makes the way so dark;
A look—a frown—neglect, friend,
    That makes one miss the mark!

A look can wound a troubled heart;
    A frown can do much harm
To one who is trying hard to win;
    Midst fears and great alarm!
Neglect can cause great heartache
    To one we really love;
We'll never know its damage
    Until we meet above!

Remember it is the little things
    That make one great or small;
A little choice can fool one
    And make one stand or fall;

For "Little foxes spoil the vine,"
They still do in our day;
So don't forget the little things;
Be sure to watch and pray!

Be kind and understanding
To your brother every day;
And you will be a blessing
To all who come your way;
Remember all the "Little Things"
You can do to lift the load
Of others as you journey down
Life's daily rugged road.

GERTRUDE STURGEON

A Society That Separates

The sense of belonging is becoming more and more difficult in the United States of America. Go back to our Pilgrim Fathers. They were very much a homogeneous group of people. They came from the same background and had pretty much the same beliefs, ideals, and practices. They lived in a community with a sea on one side and a wilderness on the other side. It was quite natural for them to have a sense of belonging.

This nation started out as a rural society. In small towns and in farming communities people felt a closeness to one another. In the last few years, though, we have crossed the line from being a rural nation to being an urban nation. Today many cities are growing. The bigger a city gets, the more impersonal it becomes. If people are going to know each other and be a part of each other, then there must be something to bring them together. More and more, our society is being built in such a way to separate people. In big cities, many people never go to church, while many others go to church. Among the church-going people there are literally hundreds of different denominations. There are Baptists, Methodists, Disciples, Presbyterians, Roman Catholics, Unitarians, Quakers, Episcopalians, Greek Orthodox, and on and on.

We are separated by our backgrounds and early training. There are those of us who have been taught a puritanical way of life. They are still greatly influenced by those teachings. There are others who are very liberal in their thinking and in the way they live. In reference to the social issues of our day, there are the liberals and the conservatives. Between the two, frequently there is a "great gulf fixed."

In our large cities we have people from practically every nation and every culture of the world. There was a day when, if a family of "foreigners" lived in our midst, they were a curiosity. Such is no longer true. Walk down any street in a large city and there will be families who grew up in Europe or the Far East, South America, or any other place in the world. They have different backgrounds, different concerns, and not too much interest in being neighborly with their neighbors.

We live in a society where the needs of people are different. We have different emotional, intellectual, and social needs.

One of the greatest influences in our society today is television. Back in a small town there was such a thing as neighbors visiting neighbors. Today, however, to go to see somebody in the evening is to interfere with their favorite television program. We find that even to call people on the telephone at night can often be a very unwelcome experience because of the television to which they are glued. The television has done very much to cause people to be withdrawn from one another. Instead of a people belonging to one another, more and more we are becoming a people of individuals.

Make One Close Friend

One might be well advised to think in terms of making one good close friend—finding one person with whom you share interests, going places, and doing things together. A second friend might then be found. Rare is the person who has as many as five close friends. Jesus, the friendliest man who ever lived, only had three close friends—Peter, James, and John. He had twelve disciples but those three were the ones who were close to Him.

One reason people who live alone feel lonelier than they should feel is that they are expecting something that just is not going to happen. We need to reconcile ourselves to the fact that we are not going to have a great number of close friends.

Another problem is the development of large corporations in our nation. These corporations have a way of transferring their people. Most of us know people who have never lived longer than two or three years in any community. Company policy transfers them from one area to another. A moving van comes and picks up their furniture and in many cases, even their automobiles. Their family takes an airplane to a city a thousand miles away. The company handles the resale of the house they are living in; they buy a new house in a new community and move in. They know they are not going to be there but two or three years, so, what's the use of breaking their necks trying to be nice to people and make friends? This just does not work. We need friends who have shared with us in our most important moments—friends who have shared our sorrows and laughed with us in our joys. More and more, friendship is becoming a lost art. If we expect to belong in this society today, we must work harder at it than any people who ever lived in America before.

Friends for the Wrong Reasons

Speaking of belonging and of friends, we can learn a lot from the friends of Jesus. In fact, we can learn a lot from the people who were *not* His friends. For example, among His friends were no prominent people who had great influence in society. He did not seek the friendship of people who could do Him favors, get Him membership in the right clubs, enhance His prestige, or make Him feel more important. There were some prominent people who came to Him seeking help, but there is no record of His going to them to enhance His own position. One reason many people do not have friends is they are seeking friendships for the wrong reasons.

Jesus did not have wealthy friends. Again, some wealthy people came to see Him, but there is no record of His seeking out wealthy people. Sometimes people seek friendships for material gain.

As you study His friends, you find that they were usually people who needed a friend. There is a lesson to be learned right at this point. The question needs to be asked, "Am I seeking friends for my good or for the good I can do?"

So we ask the question, "What could the friends of Jesus offer Him?" Not prestige, not influence, not position, not wealth. They might have offered Him advice, but as far as we know, He never asked their advice and they never gave Him any.

What Jesus' friends gave Him was their *love*. At times their love was tested and failed. But love is what He wanted most. In one of the most touching scenes in the Bible, after the Resurrection, He quietly said to Simon Peter (the one who had denied even knowing Him), "Simon, lovest thou Me?" (John 21:15–17). When one reaches the place that love and love alone is the only thing desired of friendship, it is far more likely to come. People know when they are being used for some unworthy purpose.

Jesus' friends gave Him their love but He gave them His love, also. More than that, He gave them inspiration and a reason for living. He was not their critic. After they had denied Him and He had been crucified, He rose from the grave on Sunday and that night He appeared in their midst. He would have every reason to condemn them for their cowardly behavior, but not one word of criticism crossed His lips. Instead, the first words He spoke to those disciples were, "Peace be unto you." During that brief visit with them, He said in effect, "I still want you to be My friends" (*see* John 20:19–23).

Many have visited the church of Assisi in Italy. It is truly a monument to Saint Francis. The church is big and impressive. The greatest monument to Saint Francis, however, is not at Assisi, but in a prayer he prayed that has found its way into the hearts of multitudes of people. You are familiar with it, but I quote it again. Every time we read it, it does us good. Here is the real basis of friendship.

Lord, make me an instrument of Thy peace.
Where there is hate, may I bring love;
Where offense, may I bring pardon;
May I bring union in place of discord;
Truth, replacing error;
Faith, where once there was doubt;
Hope, for despair;
Light, where was darkness;
Joy to replace sadness.
Make me not to so crave to be loved as to love.
Help me to learn that in giving I may receive;
In forgetting self, I may find life eternal.

Relationships Are Based on Emotions

Every so often one hears the advice, "Just be yourself." The question is, "Who am I?" "What *is* myself?"

To begin with, we must realize that we are emotional creatures. These emotions have great influence on our personalities. One of our emotions is *fear.* Fear causes us many times to shrink back, to fail to take a part in life when the opportunity is offered. We also have the emotion of *disgust.* We see traits in people that we do not like. Before we realize it, we get turned off from others. At the same time, we believe that they are turned off from us.

Another emotion is the *sense of wonder.* We stand in awe of certain people. It's possible even to stand in awe of all people. We thereby shut ourselves off from normal contact.

Anger is another emotion than greatly influences relationships with other people. Some of us get angry too quickly and over matters too trivial.

Self-disparagement is an emotion. This is a feeling of unworthiness that causes us to close the door between ourselves and someone or some group of which we would like to be a part.

Elation affects us tremendously in our relationships. It is one of life's strongest emotions. Every person needs to ask the question, "What do I get excited about?"

The last emotion that I mention is *affection*. This is stronger in some people than in other people. Yet every person wants to love and be loved.

Relationships with other people are based on emotion more than anything else. The seven emotions mentioned above are the dominant emotions of every person. Study them, apply them to your self and your relationships. If you want to belong, make both your emotions and the emotions of other people work for you.

Introvert or Extrovert

Introvert or extrovert—which one are you? It makes a great deal of difference as you plan your life to know what your dominant characteristics are. Through my own studies, I have come to feel that every person has some characteristics of the introvert and some characteristics of the extrovert. I have personally never known a person who is completely one or the other. It is true that in every person, though, one of the two is dominant. If we know this about ourselves, it is a distinct help in our personal relations.

In a few sentences let me name some of the qualities of an *introvert*. He or she feels embarrassment very quickly, is apt to be offensive with blunt and unkind remarks, often does not respond to humor, is not very generous, and has some difficulty in expressing thoughts verbally. The introvert is more likely to argue with someone than to compliment that person. The introvert has trouble deciding. After making a decision he or she will back out and change at the slightest provocation. This person takes offense at things that should go unnoticed, likes to work alone, and can spend hours in daydreaming. The introvert gets moody very quickly, is upset about losing, and does not like people who disagree with his or her opinion.

On the other hand, there are some very good things about an introvert, such as being very conscientious and truthful. He or she does things because there is good reason for doing them. This person strives to be fair, honest, and accurate, and is more likely to solve his or her own problems than burden someone else with them.

Then there is the person that we call an *extrovert*. The extrovert seems not to think of self nearly so much and, as the characteristic implies, he or she is "outgoing." Any humor gets a hearty laugh, any slight or criticism rarely causes embarrassment. The extrovert says what he thinks and often without thinking. He or she is inclined to agree with whatever someone says without argument. Thus on the surface, the extrovert makes friends quickly and easily. This person does not care what other people say or think, or, at least that is the impression given.

The extrovert is likely to be impulsive, not very conscientious, and live an active life. This person is rarely moody, gives little attention to details, and does not worry about losing.

The above desciptions are sketchy and brief, but there is enough there to tell us something very important. The introvert needs praise and recognition; the extrovert needs to be asked for help.

As we study the people around us we begin to see doors through which we can walk into their friendship and fellowship.

Ego

In belonging to the group there is one fundamental principle that must never be violated. It is that you must maintain both your own ego and the ego of every individual with whom you come in contact.

You are somebody—never forget that. Never stoop below what you really are. Cling to your ideals, your hopes, your basic principles. If you have to depreciate yourself to belong, then the group to which you want to belong is not worth it.

On the other hand, there are certain basic principles in dealing with other people, and the very first one is to make that person know and believe that you feel he or she is important. The very first and obvious way to accomplish this is to learn and remember the other person's name. To do this there are three simple principles involved. When you meet a person for the first time, clearly fix the name in your mind. Many times we meet people and we never hear their names. Second, repeat the name as many times as necessary to get it engraved on your mind. Third, associate that name with something else, his or her looks, business, where you met them, or something else. When a person knows that you know his or her name, a friendly response is almost certain.

Most people are good people and want to do the right thing. Is this a statement with which you can agree? Or, do you have a suspicious nature? This has a lot to do with being accepted by other people.

A very basic and important point of acceptance is to stop worrying about being accepted yourself and begin thinking about how you can make the other person feel that you are accepting him or her. One of the easiest and quickest ways to accomplish this is to begin asking the other person about his or her life, family, work, and interests and sincerely want to know the answers.

We laugh at the story of the man who said to his friend, "Have I told you about my grandchildren? "

The friend replied, "No, and I surely do appreciate it."

We laugh at this, but that sort of attitude doesn't win many friends. Listening for five minutes to someone tell about their grandchildren might pay big dividends.

Making others feel important is the surest and quickest road to acceptance into their fellowship.

Get Up and Get Going

Let me describe two people and have you decide which one you like better and with whom you would rather be friends.

One is a person who has opinions and ideas, but is also willing to listen to different opinions and ideas from another person. This person does not appear to be lazy but has energy and vitality. This one is friendly and enthusiastic and gives the impression that he or she can be trusted. In this person's makeup is a sympathetic spirit toward others.

The other person I describe is one who does not want to hear anybody else's opinion and seems indifferent to the conditions of people around him or her. This person is really timid, but to overcome the timidity, speaks loudly, is very opinionated, and gives the impression of being concerned only about his or her own hurts. This person is not one with whom you would want to share one of your own sorrows or disappointments. When you meet this person one day he or she may be very friendly and have time to spend with you. The next day, you might meet this person and he or she hardly notices you. You speak but this person hurries on.

The truth of the matter is, in the above illustration we are not thinking about somebody else, we are thinking about ourselves. There is some of both of the people described in the two paragraphs above, in every one of us. As we look at ourselves we constantly need to ask, "Am I developing the traits of the person who really has a right to be accepted and to belong?" As we see ourselves as others see us, we are on the road to solving many of our problems.

In the Bible there is the story of a man who sat thirty-eight years by the side of a pool, waiting for somebody to come along and help him get into the pool at the right moment to be healed. For thirty-eight years there was no one who ever helped him. He might be described as "a man without a friend."

One day Jesus came along, though, and said to the man, "Rise, take up thy bed, and walk" (John 5:8). Maybe some of us have sat around too long waiting for friends, when all the time we needed to get up and get going ourselves.

Good advice to each of us is that we should get up right now and get going. Start belonging.

4

The Four *D*s of Living Alone

Decision

Decision is one reason that people live alone. Many people have had the opportunity to live with someone else in marriage, as friends, as parent and child, or in some other relationship. Many people, however, decide that living alone suits their situation better. They are not unhappy about it; they do not worry about it; and often they do not take kindly to people asking them why they are living alone.

Blessed is the person who can make a decision. In J. B. Phillips's translation of the New Testament, Saint Paul is quoted as saying, "I should find it very hard to make a choice. I am torn in two directions . . ." (Philippians 1:23). We might take satisfaction in the fact that one so great as Paul would find difficulty in making a decision, because decisions have been a burden to many people.

We use the word *dilemma*. The word *lemma* means a proposition which is assumed to be true. It might be described as "something taken for granted." It is something that we accept without difficulty. It is a proposition which is assumed to be true. When you add the prefix "di" then you have two of them. That causes the problem. Many times the two "lemmas" are completely opposed to each other. You find yourself considering exactly opposite directions. To make a decision is not easy.

This is especially true for women in our society today. Some years back a woman had very few choices to make. She could get married, or be a schoolteacher, or a nurse, or a secretary. Maybe there were one or two other alternatives, but that was about all. Not so today. Women have the opportunity to enter almost every profession and occupation in life. Sometimes there is the decision between a certain career or marriage. Often that decision is not necessary, because one can have both. In some situations one may not desire both.

When our grandfathers and grandmothers grew up, life was very simple. Today we go to the grocery store. It is a big super-market. We get a basket and walk down one aisle and up another. We have many choices. If our grandparents wanted cereal, about the only choice they had was oatmeal. Today, if you want cereal you have to look over twenty-five different kinds and then decide. When our grandparents bought their first automobile, the Model T Ford was about the only practical choice. It is very different today. When you go out to buy a car you can spend a week going from one agency to another one and end up very confused as to which is the best car for you. Consider the changes in the world of art. Today, there are many new ideas of what constitutes art. What once was called dirt and filth is now called art. How and where do you draw the line?

We are constantly pushed toward one "lemma" or another. What is the best thing to do? What is the right thing to do? What is the happiest thing to do? What makes the most sense? What fits into my total life scheme? What holds the most glamour for me? To these and many other questions, oftentimes it is not easy to give a definite answer.

One of the marks of maturity is not only the ability to make a decision, but also, to accept the consequences of that decision when it is made. If one lives alone because of decision, then let that one not complain about the disadvantages of being alone. People are less prisoners of circumstances today than ever before in history. Many decisions are made for us. We did not choose when and where we would be born, what color our skin would be, or what kind of a body we would inhabit. Many of our emotional, physiological and psychological characteristics are determined before birth. We did not choose the environment in which we were born and the influences which would surround us.

After all is said and done, we need to remind ourselves that we are not robots. There is more than one gate through which we can walk.

Life is filled with choices. We are compelled to make those choices. We either deliberately decide or we decide by default. There are many people who are living alone. Perhaps they never decided to live alone. They just never decided to live with someone else.

One can decide to live alone because of his or her career. There are other reasons one can make that decision. To live with another person requires a certain amount of discipline. We are not free to do as we please when we are not alone. Living with others means we take on certain responsibilities. A mature person is one who is willing to make a decision and then live up to the responsibilities and consequences of that decision.

Sometimes we have great difficulty in knowing the answer to make to a decision. But there is always a way to get the answer. I have a silly story but I think it illustrates a good point. The story is entitled "How Would You Weigh an Elephant?"

Tso-Tso was a powerful Chinese general. He was a brave warrior, and had many friends.

One day his friend Sun-Chuan gave him a gift. What do you think it was? An elephant! Tso-Tso was happy to have an elephant for a pet, and wanted to know how much it weighed. So he ordered his men to weigh the elephant, but no one could find scales large enough to weigh such a huge beast.

Tso-Tso had a son whose name was Tso-Choong. This little boy was wise, even wiser than the men who helped his father. He told his father that he could weigh the elephant for him. So he led it to the side of a river and made it get into a strong boat. As the elephant stepped in, it was so heavy that the water came up almost to the edge of the boat. Tso-Choong marked the place the water had reached. Then he made the elephant get off, and ordered weights to be put into the boat. The boat slowly went down again, and the water reached the mark. Now they knew the exact weight of the elephant!

We all know that people shy away from decisions. We want to ride in the front of the bus, to sit in the back of the church, and walk in the middle of the road.

We need to remember there are two kinds of freedom. The freedom to do what you want to do and the freedom to do what you ought to do. A bird wants to fly; therefore, it has the freedom to fly. A fish wants to swim; therefore, it has the freedom to swim. A dog wants to bark; therefore, he barks. On the other hand, there are limits to this freedom. I might want my neighbor's automobile, but I do not have the freedom to steal it. Therefore, in many areas my freedom is limited.

The freedom to do what we ought to do really places upon us obligation. George Washington was free to live a life of ease in Virginia; instead he accepted his responsibility to go to Valley Forge. Albert Schweitzer was free to live in Europe where he was adored, but he exercised a responsibility to spend forty years healing the wounds of people in the Belgian Congo.

There are several suggestions that one might consider in making a decision. One question is, "How will I think about it later on?" There come opportunities that may never come again. We need to picture ourselves as looking back on a decision we have made and see if we are pleased with it.

A second question to ask in reference to my decision is, "Is it the best thing for me to do?" No one else can tell you this. Others can give advice and guidance but the final decision must be made in the quietness of your own conscience.

"Where will my decision lead me?" is another important consideration in deciding. It's one thing to think about today; it's another thing when I think about the road far ahead. We not only are a "self," we are an "after-self." Your highest duty is not to yourself but to your after-self. It is not towards your interests today, but your interests tomorrow.

Decisions definitely play a large part in our lives and particularly in whether or not we are going to live alone.

Divorce

Divorce is one of the major reasons that people live alone. Several years ago, I wrote a book entitled *The Sermon on the Mount*, published by Fleming H. Revell Company. Incidentally, this book on the greatest sermon ever preached is still available in the bookstores. In reading what I wrote there about divorce, I have decided that I cannot improve upon it now, so let me quote from those pages.

Ye have heard that it was said by them of old time, Thou shalt not commit adultery:

But I say unto you, That whosoever looketh on a woman to lust after her hath committed adultery with her already in his heart.

And if thy right eye offend thee, pluck it out, and cast it from thee: for it is profitable for thee that one of thy members should perish, and not that thy whole body should be cast into hell.

And if thy right hand offend thee, cut it off, and cast it from thee: for it is profitable for thee that one of thy members should perish, and not that thy whole body should be cast into hell.

It hath been said, Whosoever shall put away his wife, let him give her a writing of divorcement:

But I say unto you, That whosoever shall put away his wife, saving for the cause of fornication, causeth her to commit adultery: and whosoever shall marry her that is divorced committeth adultery (Matthew 5:27–32).

Just as Jesus went beyond murder to anger, now He goes beyond adultery to lust; then He proclaims the fact that it is not the action but the attitude—the inner thought—that counts the most. The thing we must keep in mind is: sin is a matter of one's mind and heart. Our actions are merely the expressions of our inward sin. And, of course, we all realize that our Lord was not condemning the normal human desires which God put into people. What He was condemning was the deliberate intention to lust. You remember it was Martin Luther who said,"We cannot keep the birds from flying over our heads, but we can keep them from building a nest in our hair."

To emphasize the importance of our inner thoughts, our Lord uses very drastic illustrations, and talks about "plucking out" the eye that offends us or "cutting off" our right hand when it offends. Of course, the words are not to be taken literally. If I were to cut out my tongue, it would keep me from saying wrong things, but on the other hand it would destroy my ability to say kind and helpful things. If I pluck out my eye, it would keep me from seeing the dirty and the suggestive, but also it would keep me from seeing the beautiful and the true. If I cut off my hand, it would keep me from hitting someone in anger, but it would also prevent me from extending it in a firm handclasp of friendship.

In this passage, our Lord is emphasizing the fact that we must deal sternly with our inner desires and feelings, and hold them in complete check. And how is this to be done? By saying to ourselves, "We will not think about this"? The victory cannot be gained in that way. For thirty-five years, St. Anthony lived the life of a hermit, struggling with his temptations. One night the devil took upon him the shape of a woman and imitated all of her acts before him. St. Anthony never did reach the point where he could overcome that.

Let me quote a passage from the writings of Dr. Clovis Chappell, which shows a better way: "The little schoolhouse that I attended years ago was surrounded by a great grove of scrubby black oak. These trees had a wonderful way of clinging to their leaves. When the frost killed other leaves and cut them from the boughs of the trees, these oak leaves still clung, though they were as dead as any that lay on the ground. Then came the sharp winds of winter. But, even they were powerless to break the hold of these dead leaves. Still later came the snow and the sleet and the ice, but their efforts were equally futile. But one day a wonderful surgeon clipped all those leaves away. Who was that surgeon? His name was Spring. Springtime got into the heart of these oaks and the sap rose up and the new leaves pushed out and said to the old dead leaves: 'This is my place.' And thus Christ will save us. Therefore, this I say, 'Walk in the spirit and you shall not fulfil the lust of the flesh.' "

Dr. Thomas Chalmers, the great Scot preacher, used to talk about "the expulsive power of a new affection."

Now, we come to one of the statements of our Lord that has caused untold concern in the hearts of many people. It brings up the whole matter of divorce. Is divorce ever permissible? If one has been divorced, and then marries again, is he living in sin?

Jesus said, *I say unto you, That whosoever shall put away his wife, saving for the cause of fornication, causeth her to commit adultery: and whosoever shall marry her that is divorced committeth adultery.* These words were laid down in a very definite day in which definite situations existed. In that day a woman had no rights; in the sight of the law she was merely a thing. Her husband had absolute power over her, and with just a word he could divorce her; there was no court that would protect her. Jesus would have the people know that marriage is the most sacred of all relations in life, and something not to be taken lightly at all. However, the situation to which He addressed these words has undergone a great change.

A bright and attractive young man came into my office; he was obviously very worried. He and his wife had been very happily married for some five years. One day, he read the words of Christ in reference to the marriage of a divorced person. When his wife was twenty years old, she had married another man; they lived together for about a year, and then he deserted her. He simply told her he was through and left. He gave her no support and no help in any way. After waiting almost another year, all the time being willing to take him back and try again, and hoping he would return, the woman finally decided that her marriage was over. So she went to court and got a divorce on the grounds of desertion. Sometime after that, she and the young man who came to see me met each other, and after a time, they fell in love and were married. Their marriage had been extremely good until he read the statement and became worried over it. He wanted to know if he should immediately divorce his wife, even though he loved her dearly. He felt that, in the light of Jesus' statement, he and his wife had no right to be married.

I happen to be a minister in the Methodist Church, and so I read to him the paragraph in the *Methodist Discipline,* which is our book of law, referring to the marriage of divorced persons. The paragraph reads thus: "In view of the seriousness with which the Scriptures and the Church regard divorce, a minister may solemnize the marriage of a divorced person only when he has satisfied himself by careful counseling that: (a) the divorced person is sufficiently aware of the factors leading to the failure of the previous marriage, (b) the divorced person is sincerely preparing to make the proposed marriage truly Christian, and (c) sufficient time has elapsed for adequate preparation and counselling" (1964 edition, paragraph 356).

This did not satisfy him. He felt that no church had a right to make any statement or rule in violation of the Bible. I agreed with him fully at that point, but insisted that this was not in violation of Christ's Word. "How can that be," he said, "when the matter is stated so plainly?"

I said to him, "I cannot show you any specific reference, but I can show you something better than that, and that is the Spirit of our Christ." I turned and read to him the story of the Prodigal Son, and talked about the love of a godly father who would forgive his sinful son and restore him to the home. I turned to the eighth chapter of the Gospel According to St. John, and read to him the story of a woman who was about to be stoned to death because of the sin of adultery. Together we saw how Christ dealt with her. After her accusers were gone, gently He said to her, "Neither do I condemn thee: go, and sin no more." He was saying to her, as the father of the prodigal was saying to him, "I am willing to give you another chance."

I talked to this young man about how, over and over, Jesus spoke of the fact that He came to save sinners, that He was the "Christ of Another Chance." "Now," I asked the young husband, "do you believe that Jesus would say to your wife: 'You married when you were twenty years old, and your marriage broke up. Whether it was your fault or not is beside the point. The point is that since you've been married once, you cannot be rightfully married again. If you do ever marry again, you and the man you marry will be living in sin. I forever forbid you the opportunity of another marriage, of a home, of children. You must live the remainder of your life alone.' "

We talked about it together, and we both agreed that such would not be the attitude of the Christ we knew in the Gospels. Surely, Jesus would have said to this young man's wife, "You made a mistake, but now you are sincere in wanting another chance, and I gladly give it to you."

As one minister, I cannot see any other position than the fact that even if one has failed in a marriage, if that one is sincere, and in the right spirit enters into another marriage, that marriage will have the blessing of God. I cannot feel that if one steals or lies, or even commits murder, God will forgive him, but the same God will never forgive one who has made a mistake in his or her marriage. I used to think that the words in the ceremony, "till death us do part," referred to the death of the physical body; but, across the years, after counseling with many, many people, I've come to realize that some other things can die, too. Respect can die. Love can die. Hope can die. And a marriage can die. Realizing this fact, it behooves every married couple to give their very best in keeping their marriage alive. But, sometimes, even the best efforts of one or both have failed, and the law of our land provides a way out. I do not feel that such unhappy people are beyond God's mercy.

Having said this, though, let us re-emphasize the fact that marriage is the most important relationship in one's life, and when that relationship is broken, it leaves deep scars on the person. The saddest words the Lord ever spoke were these: "The foxes have holes, and the birds of the air have nests; but the Son of man hath not where to lay his head" (Matthew 8:20). One of the heaviest burdens He bore was the fact that He did not have a home. Through the years I have tried to help many couples persevere in their marriage, and many of them have succeeded. Edgar A. Guest was certainly right when he said, "It takes a heap o' livin' in a house t' make it home."

When two people marry, they should be in love; that first romantic love is a thrilling and beautiful experience. Marriage means that two people have given themselves to each other, and decided to go the same way together. In her book *Glimpses of the Moon*, Edith Wharton has one of the characters saying: "The point is that we are married . . . married. Doesn't that mean something to you, something—inexorable? It does to me. I didn't dream it would—in just that way. But all I can say is that I suppose the people who don't feel it aren't really married."

Marriage, however, is based on more than just that "inexorable" feeling. It must be a growing experience in which two people:

> . . . share each other's woes,
> Each other's burdens bear,
> And often for each other flows
> The sympathizing tear.

That first romantic love is nothing compared with the strength of the love that grows as two people walk down life's path together.

"Adultery—Marriage—Divorce,"
from *Sermon on the Mount,* © 1956
by Fleming H. Revell Company

Sometimes divorce can be even more heartbreaking than death. I have spent many hours counseling and talking with people who have been through this tragic experience. Many times, though, divorce is the lesser of two evils. There are some circumstances when it seems that one has no other choice.

A minister friend of mine was saying to me that the marriage ceremony has the words "as long as we both shall live." He said, he would like to rewrite that sentence to read "as long as we both shall love."

I personally am not prepared to say that, I think there are times when couples should live together because of their obligations and responsibilities. On the other hand, many times I have advised couples that divorce is better than the lives they are living.

There are few people in our society toward whom I, as a minister, have more loving sympathy than one who is divorced. That person has been hurt, but, thank God, out of the hurt often rises a stronger and a better person. Life can go on, even after divorce.

Disappointment

Saint Paul wrote, "Whensoever I take my journey into Spain, I will come to you . . ." (Romans 15:24). The ambition of the greatest Christian preacher who ever lived was to go to Spain. He dreamed of that day. Instead of Spain he ended up in a Roman prison and execution. He knew the meaning of broken dreams and disappointment.

Years ago there was a popular song that went like this:

I'm waiting for ships that never come in
Waiting and watching in vain.
It seems that life's stormy sea
Holds nothing for me
But broken dreams and shattered schemes.
With each day of sorrow
I love to pretend
One more tomorrow and waiting will end.
I'm waiting for ships that never come in,
I wonder where they can be.*

There are many people today who can sing that song. I am thinking about a lady I know. She was engaged to a young man who went to fight in World War II back in the early forties. He was killed in battle thirty-five years ago. She has never found anyone else she loved and who loved her. She knows what disappointment is. Her story can be multiplied by many, many, who lived during World War II and the Viet Nam War.

In John Masefield's *The Widow in the Bye Street*, we find the picture of a widowed mother dreaming dreams of the day when her son will be able to release her from the drudgery of sewing from morn to midnight on shrouds for the dead. When the lad comes to man's estate, he finds work on the roads. He is able to give his mother some of the comforts that should be the portion of her old age. As the tale spins itself out, we find the son falling in love with an unworthy woman—a woman of the streets—once beautiful in face and figure but with the soul of a demon. Finding her with a rival, the boy kills him. The long arm of English law takes the widow's son and hangs him. The widow, broken by sorrow and disgrace, is compelled to go back to sewing on shrouds again, earning a mere pittance. Her dreams gone, the closing years of her life are bleak und lonely. It is not Spain with its castles, but the dull gray walls of life's loneliness and desolation.

* Words by Jack Yellen. Music by Abe Olman. Copyright 1919 Forster Music Publisher, Inc., Chicago, Ill. 60604. Copyright Renewal 1947 Forster Music Publisher, Inc. Used by permission.

Disappointment is not easy to bear. One of the most prominent and influential men the United States has had was a bachelor. People wondered why he never married because he had innumerable opportunities. As a young man, he was turned down by the girl he loved with all his heart. In spite of all his successes, he has never gotten over his disappointment. This has happened to many people. To be jilted by a lover is one of the deepest wounds of life. There are others who have never had a lover by whom to be jilted. Somehow, the circumstances of life have never brought this person together with someone with whom to fall in love.

Thus many people might say, "I ask and I do not receive. I seek and I do not find. I knock and the door does not open." There are several points that should be brought out. Remember that our lives are still unfinished. There is a man in the city where I live who was considered a business failure when he was sixty years old. Today he is a multimillionaire. He made all of his money after the age of sixty. He suffered many disappointments. Suppose he had decided that one of those disappointments was the end? He kept on going, no matter what happened.

One of the great preachers of America was the late Dr. Roy A. Burkhart. I heard him tell about a woman who said to him, "You know, about ten years ago you came into our house and one of the buttons on your overcoat was hanging by a couple of threads. I said, 'Let me sew it on.' And then you said, 'Oh, it has hung there by those two threads for a long time. You do not need to bother.' The woman related that for ten years she had lived by the thought that if my button hung by a few threads, she could hang on to life and purpose. She said, 'I had a couple of threads I could hang on to.' "

This brings to mind Howard Thurman's poem "One Thread."

Only one end of the threads, I hold in my hand.
The threads go many ways, linking my life with other lives.

One thread comes from a life that is sick, it is taut with anguish
And always there is the lurking fear that the life will snap;
I hold it tenderly, I must not let it go . . . .

One thread comes from a high flying kite,
It quivers with the mighty current of fierce and
    holy dreaming,
Invading the common day with far-off places and visions
    bright . . . .

One thread comes from the failing hands of an old, old friend—
Hardly aware am I of the moment when the tight line slackened
    and there was nothing at all—nothing . . . .

One thread is but a tangled mass that won't come right;
Mistakes, false starts, lost battles, angry words—a tangled mass;
I have tried so hard, but it won't come right . . . .

One thread is a strange thread, it is my steadying thread—
When I am lost I pull it hard and find my way . . . .
When I am saddened, I tighten my grip and gladness glides along
    its quivering path;
When the waste places of my spirit appear in arid confusion the
    thread becomes a channel of newness of life.

One thread is a strange thread—it is my steadying thread—God's
    hand holds the other end . . . .

Disappointment is never easy to bear. Some of our disappointments we can understand. They come as a result of our own
wrong decisions, or our failures to be the person we should be.
There are other disappointments that are apparently senseless
and certainly are bewildering. Even the greatest who have ever
lived have known this fact.

Adam, the first man, had his moment of weakness and his
bitter sentence was expulsion from the Garden of Eden. Abraham had his long-deferred hope of Canaan. Esau was deceived
by his brother, Jacob. Jacob had to wait fourteen long years for
the wife he wanted. Moses got to the border of the Promised

Land, but did not get to go inside. David dreamed of building the
temple, but he never could. There is an old spiritual which goes
like this:

> I've got to walk this lonesome valley,
> Nobody here can walk it for me—
> I've got to walk it for myself.

One who keeps walking through the dark night will eventually
come to the morning light.

In the book *White Banners* by Lloyd C. Douglas, we read these
words: "Good use of a disappointment?" [Paul asked.] "I can't
see what use you could make of a disappointment. If you can, I'd
be glad to hear about it. I've had a plenty."

"Well—a disappointment," ventured Hannah, feeling her
way, cautiously, conscious of his half-derisive grin—"sometimes
a disappointment closes a door in a person's face, and then he
looks about for some other door, and opens it, and gets something better than he had been hunting for the first time."

Your Disappointment May Be God's Appointment

Actually, when most people take an honest look at their own
lives, they are better pleased than they might expect. It is said that
Dean Inge, one of the most famous ministers in the history of
England, had a prayer that he said just before each sermon. It
went like this: "Dear Lord, this sermon of mine isn't much, but
I've worked honestly on it, and it's the best that I can do, at least
at the moment. I know that any good which comes from this
sermon will be Your doing and not mine. Please help me so to
live that I may become an increasingly uncluttered channel of
Your grace. To that end, may I think Your thoughts after You,
and speak Your Word. I love You, and I love these people
among whom I serve. That's that, God, *amen*."

Now go back and read that prayer and everywhere the
word *sermon* appears, put the word *life*. Read it while thinking of your own life, and as you reread it, don't you think

it is exactly the prayer for you?

We are not going to avoid disappointment, but there are two steps that we must take. First, we must do all we can to turn our disappointments into good. Remember the words of the Bible: "And we know that all things work together for good to them that love God . . ." (Romans 8:28).

Second, we must remember that things are not as bad as they seem. Here is a letter that was written by a college freshman to her parents:

Dear Mother and Dad: Since I left for college I have been remiss in writing, and I'm sorry for my thoughtlessness in not having written before. I will bring you up to date now; but before you read on, please sit down. You are not to read any further unless you sit down.

Well, then—I am getting along pretty well now. The skull fracture and concussion I got when I jumped out of the window of my dormitory when it caught on fire shortly after my arrival here is pretty well healed now. I only spent two weeks in the hospital, and now I can see almost normally. I only get those sick headaches once a day. Fortunately, the fire in the dormitory and my jump was witnessed by an attendant at the gas station near the dorm, and he was the one who called the fire department and the ambulance. He also visited me in the hospital, and since I had nowhere to live because of the burned-out dormitory, he was kind enough to invite me to share his apartment with him. He's really a fine boy and we have fallen deeply in love and are planning to get married. We haven't got the exact date yet, but it will be before my pregnancy begins to show.

Yes, Mother and Dad, I'm pregnant and I know how much you are looking forward to being grandparents. I know you will welcome the baby and give it the same love and devotion and tender care you gave me when I was a child. The reason for the delay in our marriage is that my boyfriend has a minor infection which prevents us from passing our premarital blood test, and I carelessly caught it from him. I know that you will welcome him into our family with open arms. He is kind and, though not well educated, he is ambitious. Although he is of a different race and religion than ours, I know your often-expressed tolerance will not permit you to be bothered by that.

Now that I have brought you up-to-date, I want to tell you that there was no dormitory fire. I did not have a concussion or skull fracture. I was not in the hospital and I am not pregnant. I am not engaged and I am not infected. There's no boyfriend in my life. However, I am getting a *D* in history and an *F* in science and I want you to see those marks in their perspective!

Yes, in spite of disappointments things could be worse.

Death

The word *death* really is two separate and distinct subjects. When we think of the word we need to ask the question, "The death of whom? Of the one I love and live with? Of myself?"

Death is something we shrink back from. We do not even want to talk about it. We do not want even to admit it exists, but it does exist. We do need to talk about it. We do need to face it. Let's take the two topics of death in order.

First, the death of one we love and live with. Across the years I've been the minister at many funerals. In the church where I am now the pastor we have an average of four funerals every week. Each one of them to me is the saddest. To stand with children as we bury their mother, or to stand with a young couple as we bury their baby are both heartbreaking experiences. Sorrow never becomes routine. Each one is a fresh and new experience, but for me the saddest is to stand with a wife or husband as we bury the one with whom he or she has lived—in whom one has found completeness—upon whom one has depended—one who has brought joy. To see a couple separated is for me just about life's hardest experience. The losing of a loved one is one of the very real crosses we must bear. When a couple is separated it brings deep inner pain. Love has grown tentacles which have encircled each other's hearts. When death comes, those tentacles are rudely torn away. Part of our own hearts are ripped out. Our emotions are deeply stirred.

When I first started in the ministry, there was an old retired minister living in one community where I was the pastor. He would assist me in every funeral service. He had a phrase that he would always use: "When you get back home today his [or her] chair will be empty." It was a phrase that would stir the emotions of people. I do not use that type of approach, but the truth is that chair *is* empty when one gets back home and it is hard to see and live with that empty chair. There is just no way to make that experience easy. In fact there are some who can not even accept it. They refuse to believe that the loved one has died and is buried. They want to keep on living as though death never occurred. I know one woman who always sets the table with a plate for her deceased husband.

On the other hand, there are those who rebel and become cynical, saying, "Why would God let this happen to me?" There are those who want to shout with Job's wife, "Curse God, and die."

Discussion of death need not be morbid. In fact it ought to be quite the opposite. If death is morbid to any one of us, it is because of our refusal to face it and take it into account. The greatest man I have ever known personally in the church was Bishop Arthur J. Moore. There may be others greater than he, but I did not know them. I knew Bishop Moore well. He was my bishop for twenty years. We came to be very close and intimate friends. It was like a father-son relationship. After his wife died he wrote this to me:

My dearly beloved Martha walked triumphantly into God's house on Monday, August 17th. You can imagine how lonely the children and I feel.

For more than fifty-eight years, her unfaltering faith, her

compassionate heart, and wise judgments have been for me an unfailing source of inspiration and courage. She was a woman of extraordinary faith. There was about her daily living a freshness of intelligence and a response to the needs of those about her, which made her life full of singing cheer. She was a woman of rare gifts, unfailing in her fidelity to her Master, her family, and to an innumerable company of friends, who stretch literally around the earth.

We who walked close by her side can never cease to be grateful for her radiant singing soul and Christlike compassion.

In these months of serious illness, her brave beauty and victorious faith were as clear as sunlight. In her final written word to those she loved best, she said, "I neither fear death, nor dread to die." In this earthly life she lived in God; now in that land where shadows never darken she lives with God. In life she held "her own" securely in her love. Now that she is away for a little while, we shall hold her forever in our undying affection and loving memory.

One of the things that worries me very much is right at this point. When I was a boy, my father was pastor of churches in small towns. When someone died every person in town knew about it. People would come to the home and bring flowers, food, love, and sympathy. At the time of the funeral all of the stores in the town would be closed. The people would fill the church. The family felt surrounded by loving and sympathetic hearts.

It is not that way today. Not long ago one of the funeral homes phoned to tell me that a man had died who was not a member of a local church. He had been listening to me each Sunday on television and his wife wondered if I would conduct the service. Of course, I was happy to do so. After dinner I got a map and located where they lived. I drove across town and knocked on her door. She was sitting there alone. She told me how she and her husband had lived together for forty-four years. Now they were suddenly separated. I spent an hour with her, talking the best I could, but I was the only person there. Nobody else came into that house. The next day there were six people at the funeral.

To me this is one of the tragedies of the impersonal society that we are building in these big cities. In life's deepest sorrows many people literally walk alone. At this point, let me emphasize as strongly as I can that God is not indifferent to our sorrows. When I was a student in seminary, one of our older professors used to say to us, "Boys, in every sermon you preach have a word of sympathy. There will be somebody who hears you who needs it." I have never forgotten that advice and I have lived up to it through all of these years. In every sermon the preacher ought to say that God knows you and that God loves you.

God spoke to His prophet and commanded him, "Comfort ye, comfort ye my people . . ." (Isaiah 40:1). It needs to be said again that God is *not* indifferent to our sorrows. I still love to sing the old gospel hymn:

> Does Jesus care when my heart is pained
> Too deeply for mirth and song;
> As the burdens press, and the cares distress,
> And the way grows weary and long?
>
> O yes, He cares—I know He cares!
> His heart is touched with my grief;
> When the days are weary, the long nights dreary,
> I know my Savior cares.

We Never Lose Our Loved Ones

Here I think we need to point out that we have not lost our loved ones who have died. Here is a little story so beautiful that I would like to reprint it here:

In October 1800 a boy named John Todd was born in Rutland, Vermont. Shortly afterward the family moved to the little village of Killingsworth. And there, when John was

only six years of age, both his parents died. The children in
the home had to be parceled out among the relatives, and a
kindhearted aunt who lived in North Killingsworth agreed to
take John and give him a home. With her he lived until some
fifteen years later when he went away to study for the ministry. When he was in middle life, his aunt fell desperately ill
and realized that death could not be far off. In great distress
she wrote her nephew a pitiful letter—what would death be
like? Would it mean the end of everything or would there be,
beyond death, a chance to continue living, growing, loving?
Here is the letter John Todd sent in reply:

"It is now thirty-five years since I, a little boy of six, was left
quite alone in the world. You sent me word you would give
me a home and be a kind mother to me. I have never
forgotten the day when I made the long journey of ten miles
to your house in North Killingsworth. I can still recall my
disappointment when, instead of coming for me yourself,
you sent your colored man, Caesar, to fetch me. I well remember my tears and my anxiety as, perched high on your
horse and clinging tight to Caesar, I rode off to my new
home. Night fell before we finished the journey and as it
grew dark, I became lonely and afraid.

"Do you think she'll go to bed before I get there?" I asked
Caesar anxiously. "O no," he said reassuringly. "She'll sure
stay up FOR YOU. When we get out of these here woods
you'll see her candle shining in the window." Presently we
did ride out in the clearing and there, sure enough, was your
candle. I remember you were waiting at the door, that you
put your arms close about me and that you lifted me—a
tired and bewildered little boy—down from the horse. You
had a big fire burning on the hearth, a hot supper waiting for
me on the stove. After supper, you took me to my new
room, you heard me say my prayers and then you sat beside
me until I fell asleep.

"You probably realize why I am recalling all this to your
memory. Some day soon, God will send for you, to take you

to a new home. Don't fear the summons—the strange journey—or the dark messenger of death. God can be trusted to do as much for you as you were kind enough to do for me so many years ago. At the end of the road you will find love and a welcome waiting, and you will be safe in God's care. I shall watch you and pray for you until you are out of sight, and then wait for the day when I shall make the journey myself and find you waiting at the end of the road to greet me."

This is the Christian's faith. Behind and beneath life it sees God's unfailing love. Beyond death, it confidently expects the new opportunities which a kind Father can be trusted to provide for all His children.

Some years ago I had the pleasure of preaching with Dr. Norman Vincent Peale and Bishop Arthur J. Moore. It was a thrilling experience for me just to be with those two men. I've already spoken of Bishop Moore. Let me say here that America has never produced a more thrilling preacher than Dr. Norman Vincent Peale. I remember well a service which he later described in a sermon. Let me quote what he said in a *Guideposts* article:

And just last year, when I was preaching at a Methodist gathering in Georgia, I had the most startling experience of all. At the end of the final session, the presiding Bishop asked all the ministers in the audience to come forward, form a choir and sing an old, familiar hymn.

I was sitting on the speakers' platform, watching them come down the aisles. And suddenly, among them, I saw my father. I saw him as plainly as I ever saw him when he was alive. He seemed about forty, vital and handsome. He was singing with the others. When he smiled at me, and put up his hand in the old familiar gesture, for several unforgettable seconds it was as if my father and I were alone in that big auditorium. Then he was gone, but in my heart the certainty of his presence was indisputable. He was there, and I know that someday, somewhere, I'll meet him again.

I could go much further with the idea of seeing our loved ones again. In fact I have a little book which has a wide sale entitled *When You Lose a Loved One.* In that little book I deal with some of the problems of life after death, such as a person being married more than once. We do know that God has worked out all the problems. We will know and love each other again.

In Dying We are Born

We have discussed the first topic of death: the death of one we love and live with. Now let us consider the second part: that it is coming to each one of us. Living alone has a tendency to heighten that fact. This thought fills many people with dread and fear.

Thomas Wolfe begins "Toward Which" with these words:

> Something has spoken to me in the night,
> Burning the tapers of the waning year;
> Something has spoken in the night,
> And told me I shall die, I know not where . . . .

Note the words *I shall die.* How shall we face this question? It is one thing to say that "everybody is going to die." It is a different experience to become aware of the fact that "*I* shall die."

The truth is, death comes in many forms. Some people die intellectually. There was a time when they were alive to new truths and great ideas, but as the years have come and gone, all of their creative thinking has died. Some people let their dreams and hopes die. Other people let their imagination die. Some die to the beauties and wonders and glories of this earth. Others let their consciences die. They reach a place where they feel no guilt, no pain over any wrong they might do. Some people die spiritually. They have no feeling about God or anything beyond the physical. A person living alone without the stimulation of others is in much greater danger of dying.

When Socrates was told that the time had come for him to prepare for his death, he made the reply, "Know ye not that I have been preparing for it all my life?" And so it must be with each of us. Whatever our condition we must come to terms with death just the same way as we come to terms with life.

On a previous page in this book we quoted the familiar prayer of Saint Francis of Assisi. Read the last line once again:

It is in dying that we are born to eternal life.

And here is that entire poem of Thomas Wolfe:

Something has spoken to me in the night,
Burning the tapers of the waning year;
Something has spoken in the night,
And told me I shall die, I know not where.
Saying:
"To lose the earth you know, for greater knowing;
To lose the life you have, for greater life;
To leave the friends you loved, for greater loving;
To find a land more kind than home, more large than earth—
Whereon the pillars of this earth are founded,
Toward which the conscience of the world is tending—
A wind is rising, and the rivers flow."

It is my firm conviction that we are living in eternity at this very moment and that death simply means the release from the limitations of this flesh and this life into a larger and fuller and a much greater existence. No right-minded person wants to die. It is normal to want to live on this earth as long as we reasonably can. It is also normal to so believe in the assurance and greatness of eternal life that death is robbed of its fear.

The assurance of death creates different reactions in different people. Some face it with sort of a dreamlike reaction. They just do not think about it realistically.

Others face it in the spirit of the man about whom Jesus told—the one who said, ". . . eat, drink, and be merry" (Luke 12:19). That means think about today and give no thought to anything beyond. There are others who have actually surrendered to the idea of dying and are just waiting for the end to come. Another reaction is to rush through each day with the thought that this may be the last day that we live and must crowd in everything that we can.

The most supportive help any person can find in reference to death is in the pages of the Bible, which is the Word of God. In several places I have seen listed a series of Bible readings to help us get a clearer idea of the meaning of death. Let me list these with the strong suggestion that they be read and considered.

Genesis 1: "In the beginning God . . . ."

Psalm 23: "The Lord is my shepherd . . . ."

Psalms 139:7–12: "Whither shall I go from thy Spirit? . . ."

Isaiah 40: "Comfort ye, comfort ye my people . . ." (v. 1).

John 11:1–46: "I am the resurrection, and the life . . ." (v. 25).

John 14:1–31: "In my Father's house are many mansions . . ." (v. 2).

1 Corinthians 15: "Now is Christ risen from the dead . . ." (v. 20).

2 Corinthians 5:1–10: ". . . absent from the body . . . present with the Lord . . ." (v. 8).

Philippians 1:20–30: "For to me to live is Christ . . ." (v. 21).

Revelation 21:1–7: "And I saw a new heaven and a new earth . . ." (v. 1).

Revelation 22: ". . . the tree of life . . . for the healing of the nations" (v. 2).

This says a lot to me:

ON LEAVING

Life
Is
A series
Of series
With no
Good-byes,
A few hellos
And a
Never ending
Pack-up
And leave
And
Pack-up
Again.
Once we have
Begun
We have already started
The finality
And we are
Forever
Ending beginnings
Amidst
Our
Almost dreams.
Always there will be
The smell
Of a daisy
Or the bite of
Cold milk
To remind us
We are
Forever
Beginners
Beginning
And blindmen
Almost
Seeing.

The fact is that sooner or later death becomes a reality. I would like to close this section with a little poem I like very much, and also from which I gain inspiration.

I dreamed Death came the other night
    and Heaven's gate swung wide—
With kindly grace an Angel came
    and ushered me inside—
And there to my astonishment
    stood folks I'd known on Earth—
Some I'd judged and labeled "unfit" and "of little worth"—
Words of indignation came to my lips
    but never were set free—
For every face showed stunned surprise—
    No one expected me . . . .

                                        AUTHOR UNKNOWN

5

Sorrows Are Precious Possessions

Some time ago I conducted the funeral service for a teenage girl. Later the mother said to me, "How long will it take me to get over this sorrow?"

I replied, "Do you really ever want to get over it?"

She quietly answered, "No."

We do not "get over" our sorrows. Sorrows become permanent and precious possessions of our lives, but—tragically—sorrows have the power to make us either bitter or better. This is what we are concerned about in this chapter.

Previously I quoted Job's wife. Let me give the entire quotation here, "So went Satan forth from the presence of the Lord, and smote Job with sore boils from the sole of his foot unto his crown. And he took him a potsherd [piece of a broken pot] to scrape himself withal; and he sat down among the ashes. Then said his wife unto him, Dost thou still retain thine integrity? curse God, and die" (Job 2:7–9).

When troubles come this is how we are apt to react at first. Our minds turn toward God with feelings that are harsh and rebellious. We are puzzled—we are resentful—as to why God would allow this to happen. We even think of God as "sending" evils upon us. More than anything else we need to Christianize our thinking about God. God does not deliberately create calamity, send disease, cause wrecks, and all the other things that hurt and destroy. When we think of the calamities of life, surely we could not love a God who is responsible for sending them.

On the other hand, the fact remains that God permits certain things to happen. In the next pages we will be dealing with the question of why He does, but I am afraid that we never come up with a complete answer. How to reconcile the sorrows, troubles, and heartaches of people with the goodness and love of God is a puzzle that has not yet been solved. The great Boston preacher, Phillips Brooks, once said that if someone should tell him how he could explain the mystery of evil, he would close his ears to the offer. He went on to say that it is a mystery that can never be fathomed. Still, we say with John Greenleaf Whittier:

> Yet in the maddening maze of things,
> And tossed by storm and flood,
> To one fixed trust my spirit clings;
> I know that God is good.

Let us emphasize that suffering and sorrow are not the results of God's disfavor. It is very important at this moment to say, "God would not take the life of one's wife or husband to punish the other one." Really, I think no one would say that, but sometimes we subconsciously feel it. Sin is not the cause of all human suffering and tragedy. We need to know that. Many of the purest saints who ever lived have suffered the deepest sorrows.

And there are some other ideas about human suffering that need to be thrown on the scrap heap. There are no ghosts, no vampires, no ghouls. Such things as heart attacks, cancer, automobile accidents, and all the other things that kill people are not punishments for sin.

Really the reason you suffer is that you have a capacity to feel. Thank God that you *can* suffer. Suppose you stuck a pin in your hand and felt no pain. That would be a very serious matter. The fact that you can feel pain is good and normal.

Oftentimes our personal integrity is at stake. Sometimes to be at peace with ourselves, we blame ourselves. It is easy to say, "I guess I was wrong or this would not have happened. I will just suffer the consequences." But to do that is to become a hypocrite.

As Jesus suffered on the cross, He did not "confess" that He was at fault. He might have said, "I failed in my life's work. Apparently I did not reveal God as clearly as I should have. Therefore, I am being justly crucified." When one is innocent, he or she must not look at suffering as punitive. I have counseled many times with a brokenhearted husband or wife who was blaming himself or herself. Actually there was no blame at all. I cannot explain why some couples live together until they are eighty years old or more, and other couples are separated in their thirties or forties and sometimes even in their twenties. There is nothing fair about innocent suffering.

Many times we say that death is not a tragedy, but many people who are reading these pages can testify that death is terribly real. As a result, grief is not only human, it is a Christian and an appropriate response.

As a minister, I have many times felt myself in the situation of a little girl who had been sent by her mother on an errand. The little girl was late in returning and her mother asked her why. She explained that a playmate of hers had broken a doll. She had stopped to help her. The mother wondered how she could fix the little girl's doll. She asked, "How did you help her?" Her reply is truly wonderful. This little girl said, "I sat down and helped her cry." Time and again in my ministry I have not been able to help the situation. The only thing I could do was sit down with somebody and help them cry.

Tears are not an indication of the lack of faith, nor are they signs of weakness. A biologist has pointed out that lower forms of life do not suffer. The earthworm merely reacts to stimuli. Maybe the earthworm does not need to be able to suffer. Doctor E. Stanley Jones once said, "If I did not have a cross, I would pray for one." Suffering develops our souls. It increases our capacity for God. It purifies our faith. At the bottom of the scale of life we see no pain. At the top of the scale of life we see the cross of Christ.

Those who are living alone because of some sorrow need to remember that your sorrow is really a beautiful memorial for your loved one.

When tragedy or sorrow comes into our life we go through several stages. The first one is comprehending that it has happened. For example, when a loved one dies, it may take weeks or even months to fully realize what has happened. Our minds resist the thought that such could have happened. We can refuse to admit it or we can become so shocked and stunned that we are unable to admit it. It takes time to realize that certain things have happened. Simultaneously, with comprehending our sorrows comes emotional expression and many times out of expression comes emotional release. As I have pointed out, it is good to give expression to our sorrows. There also comes a time when we need to dry our tears. We go through periods of self-pity—an escapism. We would like to just get away from it all. The prophet Jeremiah in a moment of anguish said, "Oh that I had in the wilderness a lodging place . . ." (Jeremiah 9:2). There is a tendency to run away—to escape.

When a person is suddenly alone, often panic and fear come. I distinctly remember my mother's saying to me after my father's death, "I cannot go on without him. I depended upon him for everything." My mother believed that, but she did go on without him. In fact, she lived twenty-five wonderful years after my father died. I remember that one of the things that bothered my mother was that she could not drive a car. She learned that she could live without driving a car. I feel that the most creative years of my mother's life were the years when she was forced to depend upon herself. She had her anxious moments, but somewhere along the way she learned the old expression, "Life by the yard is hard, but life by the inch is a cinch."

One of the normal and human reactions to sorrow is resentment. Sometimes there is even anger. We take the good events that happen to us as that which we deserve. The bad things that happen to us we resent. It is much more common to be resentful than it is to be thankful. In this spirit it is not easy for us to pick up life and go on again. Gradually we find ourselves building a new life, finding new paths, making new friends, and generally getting on with the business of living.

Gradually we realize that life has not ended for us in spite of what has happened. Little by little we begin to accept the circumstances, to adjust to them, and to make the most of them. We are not going to "get over" our sorrows, but we are going to keep on about the business of living.

"Sighs Too Deep For Words"

Saint Paul said, "Likewise the Spirit also helpeth our infirmities: for we know not what we should pray for as we ought: but the Spirit itself maketh intercession for us with groanings which cannot be uttered" (Romans 8:26). *Groanings which cannot be uttered.* There is stark realism in those words. There are times when within us there are sorrows and hurts and pain that just cannot be expressed in words.

The Revised Standard Version of the Bible softens those words a bit and makes them read "sighs too deep for words."

Most of us know what it is to groan or to sigh. It is crying without tears. It is expressing your helplessness, your discouragement, your deepest yearnings, your harshest experiences. Many of our sighs stay within our hearts. They strain for expression. They yearn for communion with others, but they are left where they are—at the bottom of our hearts.

Sometimes we sigh over the hurts of our children. Some of our sighs come as a result of the injustices of this world. We sigh for things that might have been in our own lives—but never were. We also sigh for things that were but did not have to be. Sometimes we sigh and ask, "Why?" Other times our sigh is, "Why not?"

The point is, deep in our hearts there are some feelings that just cannot be expressed in words.

Sighs Into Songs

No matter what has happened, we should not spend the rest of our lives "sighing." Sighs can be turned into songs!

In turning sighs into songs there are several steps we must take. First, it is normal to groan, to sigh, to cry. I sometimes say to people, "Tear up or you will tear up." Tears are often a preventive of tearing ourselves to pieces. The danger is that we keep on crying longer than we should. There comes a time when we need to start a new life. We never forget our deep loves of yesterday. In fact we hold them in our hearts the remainder of our lives. We do, however, accept the fact that death is death, that divorce is divorce, that disappointment is disappointment. There is a time to go on and start living. I am not suggesting that we forget, but I am saying that there are new experiences on down the road of life. We must reaffirm our belief that there is relief from grief!

There is a verse in Lamentations which can be translated to read:

> My soul is bereft of peace,
> I have forgotten what happiness is.
> Lamentations 3:17 RSV

We need to start again remembering what happiness is and also begin in reaching for as much of it as we can. Life is not over for you and it is possible for you to find some happiness. It may not be the same happiness you have lost—maybe not as much—but at least some.

An argument could be made that the word *why?* is the greatest enemy of mankind. Again and again we are moved to say *why?* but there are some people, praise God, who reach the point of discovering that life is to be enjoyed and not to be explained. Even on the cross Jesus said, "Why?" (*see* Mark 15:34). God did not answer that question. In fact, that is one question God never answers. He never answers it, because the very speaking of the word *why?* means that we are unwilling to accept the reality of what happened. We do not want an explanation. We are seeking an argument. We would not accept God's answer if He gave it to us.

Instead of asking why we have lost something, we should begin to take inventory as to what we have left. There is still some life in you. There are deeds to be done. There are people to be loved. There are things to be enjoyed. You do not need to make yourself feel guilty the next time you laugh. Plant firmly in your mind that you can keep going, no matter what has happened; that you have not lost everything, and that life goes on.

There is a poem I clipped several years ago, written by Mary Lee Hall. It says something that all of us need to hear. Listen to these words:

TURN AGAIN TO LIFE

If I should die and leave you here a while,
Be not like others, sore undone, who keep
Long vigil by the silent dust and weep.
For my sake turn again to life and smile,
Nerving thy heart and trembling hand to do
That which will comfort other souls than thine;
Complete these dear unfinished tasks of mine,
And I, perchance, may therein comfort you.

Some years ago Hannah Green wrote a novel entitled *I Never Promised You a Rose Garden*. Even if she had written nothing but the title she said a lot. Let each of us ask ourselves the question, "Who has promised me a rose garden?" The truth is that nobody has the right to make that promise. It would be a promise that could not be kept.

There are some promises of God that are truly wonderful. In just one verse the prophet Isaiah brings us three glorious promises from God. Notice these: *beauty for ashes—the oil of joy for mourning—the garment of praise for the spirit of heaviness* (Isaiah 61:3). Those are truly marvelous, wonderful promises. Really, what more could one ask? We speak of sorrow as though it were the worst thing that ever happens in a life. Frequently it may be the best thing. Often we have heard the expression,

"Troubles color life." We have also heard the rest: "We have the power to choose the color."

We frequently hear this poem quoted:

> I walked a mile with Pleasure,
> She chattered all the way,
> But left me none the wiser,
> For all she had to say.
>
> I walked a mile with Sorrow,
> And ne'er a word said she,
> But, oh, the things I learned from her,
> When Sorrow walked with me!
>
> ROBERT BROWNING HAMILTON

On the wall of the Institute of Physical Medicine and Rehabilitation in New York City there is a plaque entitled "A Creed for Those Who Have Suffered." Here is that wise inscription:

> I asked God for strength that I might achieve,
> I was made weak that I might learn humbly to obey.
> I asked for health that I might do greater things;
> I was given infirmity that I might do better things.
> I asked for riches that I might be happy;
> I was given poverty that I might be wise.
> I asked for power that I might have the praise of men;
> I was given weakness that I might feel the need of God.
> I asked for all things that I might enjoy life;
> I was given life, that I might enjoy all things.
> Almost despite myself, my unspoken prayers were answered.
> I am among men most richly blessed.
>
> AUTHOR UNKNOWN

No people on earth ever suffered longer and more than the people of Israel, yet out of their suffering came the Ten Commandments—the basic laws and ethical standards of our society today. Out of their suffering came the greatest prophets the world has ever known and even "the Suffering Servant" who is our Lord and Saviour, Jesus Christ. They were called "the chosen people," but being chosen of God did not protect them from suffering. In fact, their suffering is what made for greatness. Right now would be a good time to read again the words of George Matheson's familiar hymn:

O Love that wilt not let me go, I rest my weary soul in thee;
I give thee back the life I owe,
That in thine ocean depths its flow
May richer, fuller be.

O Light that foll'west all my way, I yield my flickering torch to
    thee;
My heart restores its borrowed ray,
That in thy sunshine's blaze its day
May brighter, fairer be.

O Joy that seekest me thru pain, I can not close my heart to thee;
I trace the rainbow thru the rain,
And feel the promise is not vain
That morn shall tearless be.

O Cross that liftest up my head, I dare not ask to fly from thee;
I lay in dust life's glory dead,
And from the ground there blossoms red
Life that shall endless be.

I go back to the thought of our worst enemy—the word *why?* The more we think about it the more we might be able to say, *"Why not?"* Instead of saying, *"Why me?"* let us get to the place where we can honestly say, *"Why not me?"* The question *"Why not me?"* may bring the very wonderful results of overcoming in your mind and life the mystery of trouble and grief, and in its stead, give you the power of love and redemption.

One of the ministers I have loved and appreciated across the years is Dr. Charles Ray Goff. He was the distinguished pastor of the Chicago Temple until he retired. I remember hearing him tell in one of his sermons a story about the old song which begins "When peace, like a river, attendeth my way"—and ends with the words "It is well, it is well with my soul." Doctor Goff explained that this song was written by a Chicago businessman by the name of H. G. Spafford in the year 1873. He said the story is almost unbelievable and yet he had checked up and found it to be true.

The great Chicago fire destroyed most of the property and wealth of Mr. Spafford. He was left almost penniless. Instead of crying over his misfortune, he and his wife set to work to take care of the people who had lost their homes during that great fire. They set up a kitchen and places to sleep. They gave themselves in trying to alleviate all the suffering they possibly could. After several weeks of trying to care for people who were the victims of that great fire, Mr. and Mrs. Spafford where almost exhausted. A kind physician said to them that they had to get away and take a trip.

Following that advice, they left for New York with their four little girls. After they arrived in New York, he received a message saying that if he came back to Chicago he might be able to salvage something from his losses. He put his family on a ship for Europe. Then he went back to Chicago promising to come to them as soon as possible. As the ship was making its way across the Atlantic, it was crashed into by another vessel and split in two. This was a major disaster of the sea. Mrs. Spafford with her four little girls were thrown out into the ocean. They tried to hold on to pieces of wreckage, but one by one each of those little girls slipped out of Mrs. Spafford's grasp and underneath the water.

Mrs. Spafford was rescued. Two weeks later she landed in Wales and sent back a cablegram to her husband in Chicago. The cablegram contained only two words: SAVED, ALONE.

As soon as he could, Mr. Spafford got to her. They gave each other loving comfort. As a result of that experience, he wrote the words of that song. After hearing Dr. Goff telling the story, I looked up the song and read the words again. It took on for me a new and significant meaning. Read what Dr. Spafford wrote as he thought about four precious little girls who were lost at sea:

IT IS WELL WITH MY SOUL

When peace, like a river, attendeth my way,
When sorrows like seabillows roll—
Whatever my lot, Thou has taught me to say,
It is well, it is well with my soul.

Tho Satan should buffet, tho trials should come,
Let this blest assurance control,
That Christ hath regarded my helpless estate,
And hath shed His own blood for my soul.

My sin—O the bliss of this glorious tho't—
My sin, not in part, but the whole,
Is nailed to the cross, and I bear it no more:
Praise the Lord, praise the Lord, O my soul!

And, Lord, haste the day when my faith shall be sight,
The clouds be rolled back as a scroll:
The trump shall resound and the Lord shall descend,
"Even so"—it is well with my soul.

Chorus:

It is well
It is well
with my soul,
with my soul,
It is well,
It is well with my soul.

We Gain Through Pain

God does not send affliction upon us, but troubles can be turned into triumphs. In the midst of the longest psalm in the Bible, this truth is affirmed. We read, "Before I was afflicted I went astray: but now I have kept thy word . . . . It is good for me that I have been afflicted . . ." (Psalm 119:67-71).

We need constantly to remind ourselves that the hard experi-

ences of life give us strength and understanding. We grow by
conquering troubles and overcoming difficulties.

An Indian philosopher gave a striking illustration of this truth.
He said: "I have on my table a violin string. It is free to move in
any direction I like. If I twist one end, it responds; it is free. But it is
not free to sing. So I take it and fix it into my violin. I bind it, and,
when it is bound, it is free for the first time to sing!"

The Christian preacher-poet, George Matheson, stricken with
blindness at the outset of his ministry, wrote:

> Make me a captive, Lord,
>   And then I shall be free;
> Force me to render up my sword,
>   And I shall conqueror be.
> I sink in life's alarms
>   When by myself I stand;
> Imprison me in Thy mighty arms,
>   And strong shall be my hand.

"When Life Tumbles In, What Then?"

Before we leave this subject let me quote from one of the most
famous sermons that has ever been preached. Arthur John Gossip was one of the great preachers of Scotland. After the sudden
death of his wife, Dr. Gossip preached a sermon entitled "When
Life Tumbles In, What Then?" This sermon has been called one
of the most influential sermons ever preached in the English
language. Here is an excerpt from that sermon:

> Further, there is a saying in Scripture, "Receive not the
> Grace of God in vain." That Christ should die on our behalf,
> that God should lavish his kindness on us, and that nothing
> should come of it, how terrible! And were it not pitiful if we
> receive the discipline of life in vain: have all the suffering of
> it, pay down the price in full, yet miss what it was sent to
> teach!

I know that at first great sorrow is an experience that stuns, that the sore heart is too numbed to feel anything, even God's hand. When his wife died, Rossetti tells us, he passed through all that tremendous time with a mind absolutely blank, learned nothing, saw nothing, felt nothing; so that, looking back, all he could say was that sitting in a wood with his head in his hands, somehow it was photographed permanently on his passive mind that a certain wild flower has three petals. That was all.

But by and by the gale dies down, and the moon rises, and throws a lane of gold to us across the blackness and the heaving of the tumbling waters. After all it is not in the day, but in the night, that star rises after star, and constellation follows constellation, and the immensity of this bewildering universe looms up before our staggered minds. And it is in the dark that the faith becomes biggest and bravest, that its wonder grows yet more and more. "Grace," said Samuel Rutherford, "grows best in the winter." And already some things have become very clear.

One becomes certain about immortality. You think that you believe in that. But wait till you have lowered your dearest into an open grave, and you will know what believing it means. I have always gazed up at Paul in staggered admiration when he burst out at the grave's mouth into his scornful challenge, his exultant ridicule of it, "O death, where is thy sting? O grave, where is thy victory?" But now it does not seem to me such a tremendous feat: for I have felt that very same.

6

Guilt—Forgiveness and Forgetting

There is a story which has been told many times about a hunter who slightly wounded a bird causing it to fall to the ground. As he lifted it up, the bird began to speak to him, saying, "Hunter, if you put me in a cage I'm going to tell people all of your secrets. It will make you miserable to have your friends know all those things about you that you would like to keep hidden. But," the bird continued, "if you will turn me loose, I will tell you three bits of wisdom that will make you both wise and successful."

The hunter was impressed and agreed to let the bird go in exchange for the wisdom.

So the bird said, "First, do not believe everything you hear. Check and test it out first. Second, do not try to do something that is beyond your limitations. Not only may you fail, but you will become an object of derision among other people. Third, whenever you make a mistake, forget it instead of grieving and torturing yourself about it. Tomorrow is another day."

The hunter then turned the bird loose. As the bird flew to a branch in a tree, it began to speak to the hunter and said, "You are foolish. You made a mistake to let me go. I carry inside of me a priceless diamond. It is so valuable it could make you many times a millionaire."

The hunter ran to the tree and tried to climb to where the bird was, but as the hunter climbed the bird would fly higher. Finally, as the hunter was reaching for the bird, he fell to the ground and broke his leg. Then the bird began talking to the hunter again. "You are a foolish person. I gave you three very wise truths, yet in just a few minutes after receiving them, you completely failed to live up to them.

"I told you not to believe everything you heard. I made a statement that there was a very valuable diamond inside of me. There is absolutely no reason why you should have believed that. Second, I told you not to try to do something beyond your limitations, yet you tried to climb a tree and catch me, which was impossible for you to do. Third, I warned you not to worry about something you could not change. Yet after turning me loose, you tried to change everything and take me again as your prisoner."

In that story we have a very wise bird and a very foolish person. We need to underscore those three very wise truths that the bird gave to the hunter.

Every Saint Has a Past
And Every Sinner Has a Future

Sooner or later every person experiences what we call guilt. We look back and remember wrong decisions that we made, harsh words that we spoke, places where we failed, opportunities we did not seize, sins we have committed, and goodness we did not obtain. To some degree every one of us has "a past" that we are ashamed of and feel guilty about. Our past has a way of staying with us, influencing our lives, bringing sadness to our hearts, and making it harder for us to get on with the business of living.

We need to realize that we cannot escape our past. Whatever it is—good or bad—that is what it is. We remember how Pilate is quoted in the Bible as saying, "What I have written I have written" (John 19:22). All of us can say that. Of course, there are many happy things in our past that we do *not* want to rub out. It is also true that "every saint has a past—and every sinner has a future."

Remorse May Be Good

There are some guilts which must be faced and dealt with or they become dark shadows over the remainder of our lives. I cannot count the times I have heard such laments as, "Why did I not call the doctor sooner?" or, "Why did I not pay more attention to him (or her) when we were together?" or, "Why did I speak those harsh words which were so unnecessary?" or, "Why did I do what I did?" This happens especially when a couple has lived together and are separated. The one left can look back with remorse.

Do not miss the value of remorse, however. It can be a cleansing and a good experience in our lives.

Thinking about past wrongs and mistakes brings to us an inner restlessness. Thoughts of the past can destroy all peace of mind in the present. Self-reproach and shame just do not go far enough, but remorse can lead us in the right direction. The first step is simple confession and repentance. It has often been said, "Confession is good for the soul but bad for the reputation," that is true and because it is the truth, there is a lot of confession that should be made to God and to God alone. There are times when confession should be made to some other person. Maybe it is a person whom you have wronged or your confession may be made to a trusted counselor.

Confession leads to amends when that is possible. If one steals money from another, many times it can be paid back. Other times, amends are not possible. Unkind words are difficult to erase and the repeating of them does more hurt than help. Maybe we failed to render services when the opportunity came, but now the opportunity is gone and there is nothing we can do about it.

There are three steps that must be taken when one feels remorse: *penitence, pardon,* and *peace.* The first one we do ourselves, the second we accept for ourselves, the third is an unmerited reward.

When we repent of some past wrong, it is the best that is within us crying out for fulfillment. It means that we turn away from that which we regret. Dante said it best, "He who repents not, cannot be absolved. Nor is it possible to repent and at the same time to will to sin, the contradiction not permitting it." True penitence is our intention to embrace what is good and to live the best we can with God's help by those virtues which are highest.

Sorrow over the past is a recognition that we have done wrong—that perhaps we have pained someone else and certainly ourselves. True penitence will kill impulses to evil which are alive in our hearts.

Do not be sad that you feel sorry about something in the past. Be glad that you feel sorry.

William L. Sullivan said it beautifully, "There is in repentance this beautiful mystery—that we may fly fastest home on a broken wing."

The *inability* to repent is probably the worst imprisonment that any person can experience. The *ability* to repent means that there is the possibility of freedom—to turn "right about face," to change your mind—and most importantly—to start a new life.

There is an old story of a man who stopped at a country store to ask the distance to a certain town. The reply was, "If you continue in the direction you are going, it will be about twenty-five thousand miles, but if you turn around, it will be about three miles." Repentance means the freedom to turn around. That is glorious and wonderful.

Most importantly, repentance leads to forgiveness. That is our next subject.

Forgiveness

In one of his lighter moods, the famous Thomas Hood wrote the jingle:

> Lives of great men oft remind us
> As we o'er their pages turn,
> That we too may leave behind
> Letters that we ought to burn.

As I have been saying, all of us have some deeds that we wish had never happened or that could be blotted out.

Forgiveness is a three-fold proposition: there is the forgiveness of God, the forgiveness of others, and the forgiveness of ourselves.

First, I can assure you of the certainty and the reality of the forgiveness of God. In the Bible we read that ". . . God is love" (1 John 4:8). In this sense the words *love* and *forgiveness* are really synonymous. We are aware of the fact that there are three Greek words for love: *eros*, *phileo*, and *agape*. *Eros* means only the physical side of love. The Greeks use the word *phileo* to refer to human relations and its real meaning is *respect*. The word *agape* means *love given when it is not deserved*. Literally it can be translated "forgiveness." There is a wonderful statement in the Bible: ". . . for I will forgive their iniquity, and I will remember their sin no more" (Jeremiah 31:34). That means that when God forgives, it is eliminated from His mind. It exists no more. It is completely forgotten. Forgiveness is nonjudgmental love. That means love in spite of everything else.

From the very beginning forgiveness means that you should extend it to any person in the past or present. It means that you accept it from any person in the past or present. Having done those two things, you prove it by forgiving yourself. It may be that there is something that you remember, but you certainly do not remember it against yourself. Forgiveness eliminates your own bitter memories and your self-hate. In fact forgiveness eliminates much of the loneliness of life. We are lonely oftentimes because we condemn and criticize ourselves too severely. As a result, we feel inferiority. Inferiority leads to withdrawal. Living by ourselves makes forgiveness one of our strongest imperatives.

I have a poem that I have had a long time about the difference in the feelings of men and women. I think it is wonderful. I do not know its source, but it goes like this:

"What a man do don't trouble him none,"
Says Piney Woods Pap a smilin'.
"What a woman do she's agoin' to find out,
Or set the place a bilin'.
A woman that loves a man sezee
Won't never change nur vary;
No matter how onery low he gits
A woman's that contrary.
A woman's jes natchelly got to be good
Or git all stained with sin,
But a man jes ups and sheds it off
Like a snake sheds off its skin.
A woman prays about the wrong she does
Until it sounds like double,
But a man jes ups and forgives himself
And saves the Lord the trouble."

Let me try to say at this point what forgiveness is and what it is not. First, what it is NOT: Forgiveness is not *forgetting about it*. Many times we will remember things as long as we live. Just to say, "Forget it!" is not forgiveness.

Neither is forgiveness *overlooking another person's behavior*. Sometimes we can tell ourselves to pay no attention to what the other person says or does, but that is not forgiveness.

Along this same line, forgiveness is not *tolerating things that we cannot accept*. Certain people have thoughts that are beyond our point of toleration.

Neither is forgiveness *excusing evil*. There are some things that are right and some things that are wrong. We have our principles and to say merely, "Nobody's perfect" is not forgiveness.

Many times forgiveness is *undeserved*. If we wait until we feel a person deserves to be forgiven, we may wait until the day we die.

Finally, forgiveness is not a *feeling*. We can feel things but not act upon them. Forgiveness is something we *do* in spite of our feelings.

So we ask the question, "If forgiveness is not this and that and the other, then what is it?" First, forgiveness is *deciding whether or not our love for the other person is greater than the hurt that has been done to us.*

Forgiveness is *believing that another person can change and not repeat the same thing again.*

Forgiveness is *more concern about the relationship with another person than about the deed to be forgiven.*

Forgiveness *refuses to accept evil as "human."* It believes that evil degrades people; therefore forgiveness loves the person even though the actions of the person are despised.

Forgiveness *has no strings attached to it.* It is not something that we plan to do tomorrow or under certain conditions. It is something that is done now.

Forgiveness means *that the relationship is restored.*

Many who are reading these words are thinking of some person who now is beyond our reach. Forgiveness can apply even when two people are no longer together. That is important and essential. Whether the other person is there or not, forgiveness is something that you, yourself, can experience and practice.

Grief is one of the most intense of all the emotions. It has the power to create extreme shock. In such a condition no person is able to think clearly. One of the mistakes a person who is in grief-shock makes is to go back and remember some misunderstanding with a loved one, to recall some angry words or criticism, to remember some things that were left undone. What we need to do is to remember that we lived together as imperfect human beings. Unhappy words, impatience, neglect, and the like were all part of the normal give-and-take of living. God forgives. All of us need forgiveness. Most importantly, we need to forgive ourselves. Let us take comfort in these words of the psalmist, "If thou, Lord, shouldest mark iniquities, O Lord, who shall stand? But there is forgiveness with thee, that thou mayest be feared" (Psalms 130:3, 4).

The Pathway to Forgiveness

Here let me very briefly give the pathway to forgiveness. Turn to the Bible and you will find that there is only one source of forgiveness. It is not the mountains, however great their grandeur, because mountains can not forgive. It is not the vast ocean, as mighty as it is. Its tides have no power to wash away our guilt. There are some other things that do not have the power to forgive, such as a day in the country for relaxation; jogging two miles every afternoon; a bottle of pills (no matter what is their brand); and not even a bottle of alcohol. Where can we find forgiveness? Not in the office of the psychiatrist or even in a hospital bed. The only place that forgiveness can be found is with God. God is the one great Forgiver in the universe.

If anyone wants forgiveness, then the steps to follow are summed up in one glorious verse in the Bible. This is it: "If my people, which are called by my name, shall humble themselves, and pray, and seek my face, and turn from their wicked ways; then will I hear from heaven, and will forgive their sin, and will heal their land" (2 Chronicles 7:14).

First, *humble ourselves.* Pride blocks out forgiveness. Humility means having the courage to look honestly at ourselves as we really are. This means to admit the truth about our own lives.

And pray is the second step. Prayer is talking with God about our need of forgiveness. It is being willing to discuss our sins and our failures. In this prayer, we are willing to face up to the wrongs of our own lives. One of the wrongs that we need to face is our own unwillingness to forgive. Don't ask God to do something for you that you are not willing to do yourself.

And seek my face is the next step toward forgiveness. That is, as Brother Lawrence put it, "to practice the presence of God." To seek His face is to seek His fellowship. When one feels guilt, the tendency is to hide from God.

And turn from their wicked ways is the next step. Here is the proof of our sincerity. There are some things we are doing that we ought not to stop doing. There are some actions that we did in the past that we can do nothing about now. However, we can recognize that they were wrong. In that recognition we are turning away from them.

After we have taken this step, we have the promise that God will hear us, forgive us, and heal us.

All of this promise was signed and sealed in Jesus Christ on the cross.

We Must Believe It

One other point about forgiveness is that we must accept it. I can tell you about a couple who had a very serious disagreement. One spoke very harshly and unkindly to the other one. Actually this person did the other one a gross injustice. The other person was deeply hurt.

After a period of time, the one who had done the wrong went to the other one and humbly and sincerely said, "Look I made a grievous error and I am wrong. I sincerely ask you to forgive me." Very quietly and sincerely the other person said, "I do forgive you; you can believe it with all your heart."

For the next several days the person who had done the wrong kept doing little extra things for the other one: bringing little gifts, doing little favors, saying more kind words than normal. Finally the other person said, "You do not have to continue doing these extra things, I really have forgiven you."

Some people can not believe it, even though they have been forgiven.

Forgetting

Here is a little poem that I think is beautiful.

> Into my heart's treasury
> I slipped a coin
> That time cannot take,
> Nor a thief purloin—

Oh, better than the minting
Of a gold-crowned king,
Is the safe-kept memory
Of a lovely thing.

SARA TEASDALE
"The Coin"

Memory is both beautiful and glorious but memory can also be tragic. There are some events and thoughts that we need to stop remembering. Again and again I have said to people who have come to me for counseling, "Don't tell me anything you may later regret that you told." There are some topics that just do not need to be discussed. When I was in college I majored in psychology. Even in that day I vigorously disagreed with some of the teachings of Freud on the idea that we ought not to "repress" anything. My convictions are much stronger in reference to this point. Many subjects ought to be left alone. They do not need to be brought up and discussed again. I deplore the constant seeking for hidden reasons and motivating factors as to certain past actions. I think a lot of the so-called psychoanalysis might be left off. I am not thinking so much of keeping deeds and thoughts secret, as I am urging to stop thinking about them.

One must learn to live with what cannot be changed. As we look back in our past lives there are some events that are fixed and nothing can be done about them. Why worry about them or why even think about them? Whether we like it or not we are forced to live with our own past. Why not learn to do it gracefully and even happily? Do not let some unhappy memory take away the incentive of the desire to live in the present.

Close the Gate

Many times I used to visit my older brother, Stanley F. Allen, who lived in Goodman, Mississippi. He has now gone to heaven and I miss him very much. When I would visit him, he enjoyed driving me out to his farm. I soon caught on, and I would say to him, "Stanley, I think I will pass up visiting the farm. Let's just sit

here and talk." The reason is that he kept many cattle on his farm
and he had a large number of fences. It seemed that about every
hundred yards there would be a gate to open. I would get out
and open the gate, let him drive through and then close the gate
behind us. I spent most of my time opening and closing gates.

Back through the years each of us has opened and walked
through a lot of gates. My suggestion now is that we need to close
some gates—and let them stay closed.

There is great wisdom from these words of Saint Paul,
". . . but this one thing I do, forgetting those things which are
behind, and reaching forth unto those things which are before, I
press forth the mark for the prize of the high calling of God in
Christ Jesus" (Philippians 3:13, 14).

7

Growing Older

One of the classic poems of all time is Robert Browning's *Rabbi ben Ezra* in which he said:

Grow old along with me!
The best is yet to be,
The last of life, for which the first was made.
Our times are in his hand
Who saith: "A whole I planned,
Youth shows but half; trust God; see all, nor be afraid!"

It is both beautiful and comforting to say, "Grow old along with me." To have someone with whom to grow old is probably life's greatest prize. To be denied this is probably life's heaviest cross. One of the frightening experiences of living alone is right here at this point. If we are not careful, our imaginations can make us miserable.

A woman was talking with me recently. She said, "I am now sixty-three years old. I am in good health. I have a number of enjoyable activities. And each day for me is reasonably full. From time to time I visit my children and they visit me. I see their lives being filled with their work, their children, their social activities, and their businesses. Really I see no place in their lives for me. I have no one else. The thing I see for me in the future is to end up in some nursing home alone and forgotten. I do not mean literally forgotten. My children would never do that to me, but I know that

days for them could slip by very rapidly without ever having time
to come to see me. I can imagine even a month going by and
never seeing one of my children. It is a dreary prospect to antici-
pate."

I suspect that person was expressing the fear and the dread of
many people who live alone. If we could just say, "Grow old
along with me," but we can't say it because there is nobody with
us.

We might think, "Of course, Robert Browning could write
those words, but he had his beloved Elizabeth." The truth is,
when Browning wrote "Grow old along with me," Elizabeth had
been dead for three years. The great poet's life was shattered.
During those three years he had accomplished very little. At that
time he was well past the age of fifty. He wanted to run away and
hide, but he faced up to his own character and felt that he should
be more a man than a coward. He began thinking of one whom
he had admired for many years, the twelfth-century scholar,
Rabbi ben Ezra. Among other things Rabbi ben Ezra had
preached, "Approach the twilight of life with joy and hope. Approach the last of life with eagerness, not gloom. For the last of
life is the best of life. Trust God and be not afraid."

Browning was inspired to write a poem on the teachings of
Rabbi ben Ezra. He gave himself completely to it. Many of us feel
it became his crowning effort.

The point is that he was *alone* when he wrote "Grow old along
with me."

That gives some of us more assurance and inspiration.

The Ages of a Life—Seven Years at a Time

A year has four seasons, but human life has many seasons or
many ages. Let us look briefly at life's various ages.

Up to seven years is the age of infancy. During this period one
should learn security and love. Tragically, many children do not
feel love or secure during this time. If that is the case, the effects
are very difficult ever to overcome.

Between the ages of seven and fourteen, one is thought of as a

child. During this period one should learn to accept responsibility
and to cooperate with other people.

From fourteen to twenty-one is the time of adolescence. Then
one becomes himself or herself, experimenting with this personality and that personality, discovering one's physical self and, in a
sense, one's freedom to be one's self.

The years from twenty-one to twenty-eight are normally years
of very significant beginnings and attainments—the beginning of
a career, marriage, children, of becoming really adult.

From the age of twenty-eight to thirty-five is the time of extending our purposes and making firm our lives.

.During the years between thirty-five and forty-two we begin to
react to the changes of life.

Age forty-two to forty-nine is a time of rebuilding, readjusting,
recuperating. These can be our extra good years. We remember
the book, *Life Begins at Forty*. On the other hand these can be
the years when there are more crack-ups.

From forty-nine to fifty-six years is the period of transition from
physical to mental. During this period we many times make our
greatest spiritual growth.

From the age of fifty-six to sixty-three we find inspiration for
new work. During this period many people come to the fork in
the road. One road leads to retirement, the other road leads to
our most creative period. During this period is the danger of
giving up for lack of purpose.

For many the age from sixty-three to seventy are the most
mentally and spiritually productive years in life.

Life certainly need not end at seventy. Longfellow wrote some
of his finest poems after he was seventy years old. Michelangelo
was still producing masterpieces when he was nearly ninety years
old. Goethe wrote the second part of *Faust* when he was eighty-
two years old. Such a list could be endless. Many of life's greatest
achievements come after the age of seventy.

You will notice, in the above ages of life, I have divided the
years into seven. It seems to me this is the way that life falls. I
sometimes think that instead of counting the years as we do, we

should count them by sevens. Therefore, a child of seven would be one, and a person of forty-nine would be seven, and one at seventy would be ten years old.

You can divide life into two major divisions. The years under fifty are the years of physical as well as mental vitality. The years after fifty also are years of mental vitality, and also greatly increased spiritual vitality.

Space does not permit detailed discussion of each of these ages, but one I would especially like to emphasize is the age of thirty-five to forty-two. This is a difficult time for many people living alone. The idea of not being married has become real to some who anticipated it. Divorce has taken its toll at this period. One begins to be fearful that the idea of being single is not a good thing. Yet there may be, in many cases, no other alternative. During this period the question begins to arise, "What will I do when I get old?" This is the age when we face the facts of our own lives. When we stop blaming somebody else for our own mistakes. When we outgrow making excuses.

Or, look at the age of fifty, which I consider sort of the dividing line. It is really the time of new birth—the time to start new hobbies—develop new interests—even begin new careers. On the other hand, it can be the beginning of the "shriveling-up" era of your life. Diseases can become more prominent. You can begin to think of yourself as being weaker and sicker. It can be a time of giving up instead of growing up.

Now, we come to the time of retirement. *Retirement!* We can think of ourselves as "rocking-chair" cases. On the other hand, remember Thomas Edison created the electric-light bulb in his middle sixties. This really is the time to get new ideas—the time to re-tire. It's the time to forget about that big rest and begin tuning in on the millions of ideas in this glorious universe.

Beyond sixty-three can be mental and spiritual growth that we have never known before. Out of a ripened intellect can come our greatest ideas, our deepest understandings, our finest joys. These are the years that prove how you have lived and what you have put in that life. Never believe that you must dry up and bend over at the age of seventy. Above all things at this age get happiness. It is the most wonderful of all lifesavers.

Age is like a mountain high;
Rare is the air and blue—
A long, hard climb and a little fatigue—
But, oh! What a wonderful view!

AUTHOR UNKNOWN

Steps to Self-confidence

Whatever your age, one of the first things you must do is gain self-confidence. All of my adult life I have been a student of Abraham Lincoln. I believe he is the greatest American who ever lived. If you really know Lincoln, you know that his greatest problem was that he had doubts about himself, doubts which lasted until he died. Self-confidence was very difficult for him to attain, but he won out over his doubts and they never defeated him. Here let me point out some steps to real self-confidence, no matter what your age is.

First, *set for yourself a major goal in life.* Forget about the fact that you have achieved goals or that you have failed. Begin right now and get yourself a new target.

Start saying to yourself and keep on saying it until you really believe it, *"This which I have decided to do, I can do."*

Do not overly worry about making decisions. Even if you make a mistake, it can be corrected.

Talk about your fears to somebody else. Just the expression of your fears tends to overcome them.

Do not forget how to laugh. Laugh both at yourself, at other people, and at your world.

Remember that other people have the same doubts, worries, and problems that you have. Be sympathetic, kind, and thoughtful of others.

Not only should you think of what you can do for yourself and what you can accomplish, but also *perform some act of kindness that will bring strength and courage to some other life.*

Finally, and most importantly, *remember that you are never alone.* Even if your loved ones are too busy for you, or if you have only a few friends, there is a Power that we can feel and use through frequent prayer and meditation.

Here is a good place to learn a poem that has been a blessing to many, many people:

> Let me grow lovely, growing old—
> So many fine things do:
> Laces, and ivory, and gold,
> And silks need not be new.
> And there is healing in old trees,
> Old streets a glamour hold;
> Why not I, as well as these,
> Grow lovely growing old?
>
> KARLE WILSON BAKER
> "Growing Old"

In the book *Windswept,* by Mary Ellen Chase, we read these wonderful lines: "Folks say," said Mrs. Haskell, "that you can't begin life over again at sixty or thereabouts, but I've never been one to harken overmuch to what folks say. Seems though I've been startin' a new life, so to speak, all of my days . . . . One more new life ain't goin' to put me out a mite."

Appreciate Growing Older

Why don't we just accept the fact that we are growing older and stop worrying about it! Getting old is a lot better than the alternative—being dead. Let's begin by learning to appreciate ourselves as we grow older. In so doing, we will influence society to appreciate older people. Here I'll quote a story from Simone de Beauvoir's *The Coming of Age.*

In Bali it is said that once upon a time the people of a remote mountain village used to sacrifice and eat their old men. A day came when there was not a single old man left, and the traditions were lost. They wanted to build a great house for the meetings of the assembly, but when they came to look at the tree-trunks that had been cut up for that purpose no one could tell the top from the bottom; if the timber were placed the wrong way up, it would set off a series of disasters. A young man said if they promised never to eat the old men any more, he would be able to find a solution. They promised. He brought his grandfather, whom he had hidden; and the old man taught the community to tell top from bottom.

Suggestions for Growing Older

If we continue to live, we need to learn the art of growing older. Here let me make some constructive suggestions.

First, accept the fact that changes can be assets. Malcom Ross wrote a book entitled *The Man Who Lived Backward.* That is symbolic of a lot of people—but you can't live backward.

Second, each period of life has its own set of problems, but also definite assets and compensations. For example, if our physical bodies slow down, our spirits can become more alert. For every loss, as you grow older, there can be found a compensating gain—if we look for it.

The third point: faith can develop maturity. Usually we turn around and say that maturity develops faith, but it works both ways. The truth is, what we are today we become more so tomorrow. The faith we have now can be stronger as the days go by. It is a glorious thing to develop into a fully matured person.

Here are some marks of maturity.

The mature person

- Does not resent criticism—
- Knows that self-pity is futile—
- Has learned the art of temper control—
- Does not go to pieces in emergencies—
- Accepts responsibility for decisions—
- Has the patience to wait when delays occur—

- Learns to lose without undue disappointment—
- Does not worry about goals that cannot be attained—
- Is not a show-off—
- Congratulates others—
- Has learned to listen when others speak—
- Is not unduly critical—
- Makes reasonable plans—
- Accepts the fact of the existence of God.

If the above statements—or most of them—apply to you, then you are a mature person. Along this line, here is a beautiful prayer for each of us as we grow older.

Lord, Thou knowest better than I know myself, that I am growing older, and will some day be old.

Keep me from getting talkative, and particularly from the fatal habit of thinking I must say something on every subject and on every occasion.

Release me from the craving to try to straighten out everybody's affairs.

Keep my mind free from the recital of endless details—give me wings to get to the point.

I ask for grace enough to listen to the tales of others' pains. Help me to endure them with patience.

But seal my lips on my own aches and pains. They are increasing, and my love of rehearsing them is becoming sweeter as the years go by.

I dare not ask for improved memory, but for a growing humility and a lessening cocksureness when my memory seems to clash with the memories of others.

Teach me the glorious lesson that occasionally I may be mistaken.

Keep me reasonably sweet. I do not want to be a saint—some of them are so hard to live with—but a sour old woman [or man] is one of the crowning works of the devil.

Make me thoughtful, but not moody; helpful, but not bossy.

With my vast store of wisdom, it seems a pity not to use it;
but Thou knowest, Lord, I want a few friends at the end.
Give me the ability to see good things in unexpected places,
and talents in unexpected people. And give me, Lord, the
grace to tell them so.

Amen

AUTHOR UNKNOWN

"The Best Is Yet to Be"

Really you may not be as old as you think you are. Is the age of
fifty old? John Wesley thought so because, as he approached the
half-century mark, he very gloomily and hastily wrote his
obituary that he might be remembered among men, but at the
age of eighty-eight he was still living a joyous and a full life. At
that age he was not worrying about being remembered by others,
but was thinking about how he could accomplish the will of
God.

Is the age sixty-five old? Charles Elliott, president of Harvard,
once thought so and was telling a friend that he expected to die
pretty soon because of the old age he had reached. Yet at the age
of ninety-two he was living a more useful life than he was at the
age of sixty-six.

The point is, you may not be as old as you think you are. It has
been well said, "Age is only a matter of the mind! If you don't
mind, it doesn't matter."

Doctor Albert Schweitzer worked creatively and happily well
past his ninetieth birthday. He had many accomplishments he
could point to. He could have "rested on his laurels," but he
continued to believe that there were useful tasks which he could
perform. Even at the time of his death, he was working on the
manuscript for a new book.

Go back to Robert Browning's beautiful poem: "Grow old
along with me! The best is yet to be." In the beginning of this
chapter I emphasized the idea of having somebody with whom to
grow old. At this point, let's emphasize the next line and really
believe, that "the best is yet to be." No matter what your life is,

believe that your present age is the best age. And it is very likely
to be.

We love the story of Jesus at the marriage in Cana of Galilee. It
points out that He enjoyed associating with people. The story
also points out His miraculous power to turn water into wine. In
addition there is a powerful message in this story for people who
are growing older. Let's read again these words, "Every man at
the beginning doth set forth good wine; and when men have well
drunk, then that which is worse: but thou hast kept the good wine
until now" (John 2:10).

We think of youth as the good days of life. Not so in the plan of
God. God saves the best wine until last. The best years of our
lives, in God's plan, are the last years. The tragedy is we do not
believe that. We give up; we quit; we fail to live up to our opportunities. Many older people ought to be ashamed of themselves.

Earlier in this chapter we mentioned about children being too
busy for their parents. That is the way life is set up. The flow of life
is from parent to child. Not from child to parent. Let the parent
understand that and quit depending on the child. Keep on living
one's own life.

The Friend of the Aged

Let's conclude this chapter with "Beatitudes for the Friend of
the Aged":

> Blessed are they who understand
> My faltered step and palsied hand;
> Blessed are they who know that my ear today
> Must strain to catch the things they say;
> Blessed are they who seem to know
> That my eyes are dim and my wits are slow;
> Blessed are they who looked away
> When coffee spilled at the table today;
> Blessed are they with a cheery smile
> Who stop to chat for a while;

Blessed are they who never say,
"You've told me that story twice today";
Blessed are they who know the way
To bring back memories of yesterday;
Blessed are they who make it known
That I'm loved, respected, and not alone;
Blessed are they who ease the days
On my journey Home in loving ways.

AUTHOR UNKNOWN

8

When Trouble Comes

Sometime ago I was talking with a very distinguished minister who is now retired. He told me that he is eighty-seven years old, and ever since he learned to read he has read at least one chapter of the Bible every day. Most days he read several chapters. He had read entirely through the Bible a number of times. I asked him, "Having spent so much time reading the Scriptures, what is the one verse that you would pick out as your favorite?"

I could hardly wait to hear his answer. Here was a man who had lived more than eighty years with the Bible, who knew it, as the saying goes, "from cover to cover." He hesitated about replying. (During that time I thought of several of my own favorite Bible verses. I was trying to decide which one particular verse I would say is my favorite.) Finally he said to me, "You will find my favorite Bible verse fifteen or twenty times, scattered through the Bible." He said, "And it came to pass . . ." (Exodus 12:41, Acts 27:44 and many other places).

I really was shocked and disappointed. I said, "Do you mean to tell me that—in all the Bible—that one dangling phrase, 'And it came to pass,' is your favorite verse?"

As he answered me, I felt like I was being rebuked. "Let me tell you that there is no verse in the Bible that can help you more than this." He went on, "I have lived long enough to know the truth of that phrase, 'It came to pass.' All the miseries of life come to pass. Even the joys of life come to pass. All the heartaches, the troubles, the wars, the crime—all come to pass.

"A baby is born in your home, but the baby grows up and becomes a man or woman. It came to pass. You have your job, your work in life, but it came to pass. You marry and live with someone whom you love more than you love yourself—but it came to pass. There is an old song entitled 'Count Your Many Blessings,' but they all 'came to pass.' "

I started thinking about some of the happenings in my own life that I worried about—some of the events that I felt were very hurtful and that maybe I would not get over. Now, as I look back, I realize, "It came to pass." I thought about some of the occurrences that I thought were of the utmost importance, but now they are not important at all. They "came to pass."

This also applies to so many delightful and pleasurable experiences. We need to learn how to enjoy what we have when we can enjoy them, because all of the pleasures of life eventually "come to pass."

If today you feel heavy burdens and heartache—if you feel that tomorrow is hopeless—if you feel that you do not have the resources, the strengths to make it in life—just remember, "It came to pass." Nothing came to stay. Tomorrow will be a new day with a new chance, new strengths, and new opportunity. If you can really believe "it came to pass," then all despair in your life can somehow be taken away.

"It came to pass."

Life Is Short

As we go along through life, we are going to have some troubles. Not long ago I heard someone telling a story of a lesson that he learned from a hitchhiker whom he had picked up. They came to a place where a new highway was being built and there was a long detour over a rough, dusty road. The driver of the car began fretting over the conditions. He expressed his disgust and frustration. After a while the hitchhiker said, "Mister, don't sweat the small stuff!" The driver later said that this was a wonderful lesson to him. He quieted down, relaxed, and enjoyed the trip. He went on to say that since that day he has found himself often repeating, "Don't sweat the small stuff."

There is another story that I like. It is about a woman who, many years ago, took her first journey on a train. As soon as she reached her seat, she began fumbling with the window to be sure that she got exactly the right amount of air. Then she pulled the window shade up and down until she got exactly the right amount of light coming in. Then she worked with her baggage to get it placed just right. Then she took off her hat and was very careful to put it where it would not get mashed. Then she took her mirror and comb and combed her hair to be sure it was just right.

Just about the time she got everything fixed and settled down comfortably, the conductor called out her station. As she got off the train she said, "If I had known the trip was going to be so short, I would not have fussed so much over unimportant de- tails!" That is a great story for all of us. Even at its best, life is a short experience. Many of the details we "fuss over" are not worth it. If we really knew how short life is, there are many things that would be for us very *un*important. On the other hand, there are some other things that we put off and neglect that would be very *important*.

Those of us who are living alone are more apt to be worrying about things that do not matter, when we consider how short the journey really is.

Your Five Fingers

There is a phrase in the Book of Job that reads, "Yet man is born unto trouble, as the sparks fly upward" (Job 5:7). Sooner or later every person experiences some kind of trouble. Life is not always trouble, crisis and hardship. In fact, most of life is relatively quiet. I feel that there is more happiness and joy in life than there is disaster and trouble. Yet all of us who have lived many years know that there is enough trouble in life that we should consider it and learn how to handle it.

Trouble comes in many forms: it may be an illness; a marriage that has gone sour; a parent trying to bridge the generation gap with a child; disappointment in one's work; some deep sorrow; an automobile accident; a financial loss, or betrayal by a friend.

It may be that your trouble has been harsh criticism or unjust judgment. Maybe your trouble is just sheer boredom. Maybe life has lost its meaning. The point is, trouble comes in many forms, in many ways, but it eventually comes to every person.

The main question is "What do you do when trouble comes?"

I have before me a sermon by one of my friends. He is a minister I deeply appreciate and respect, Dr. Emerson S. Colaw, pastor of the Hyde Park Community Church in Cincinnati, Ohio. This sermon was published in a magazine called *Pulpit Preaching* in July, 1970. (Incidentally this is a magazine that I began more than thirty years ago and is still being published.)

I want to paraphrase some of Dr. Colaw's sermon. He tells of how Moses was troubled, wondering how he was going to lead his people out of Egypt. The Lord asked him a question: "What is that in thine hand?" (Exodus 4:2).

Whenever you are in trouble, look at your hand. It can symbolize the faith you need to handle trouble. The hand has five fingers. Let each finger stand for one of the weapons you need in facing trouble.

The first finger stands for *facts!*

You remember how, in the First Book of Kings, Elijah is running for his life from Jezebel, the king's wife. He finds a hiding place and begins to complain that he is the only person left to worship God. The Lord corrects him by saying that there are "seven thousand in Israel, all the knees which have not bowed unto Baal . . ." (1 Kings 19:18). He had seven thousand on his side that he did not know about.

When some trouble comes into our lives, we tend to magnify the power of the trouble and to depreciate our own strengths. Before we surrender to hopelessness let us be sure we have the facts.

The second finger stands for *action.*

God does many things for us, but He expects us to do some things for ourselves. Our actions prove our faith. Do you re-

member the story of Jesus' healing the lepers? He said to them,
"Go and show yourselves to the priests" (Luke 17:14 RSV). He
could have healed them with a word, but He wanted them to
prove their faith by doing something. Then we read, "And it
came to pass, that, as they went, they were cleansed."

Underscore that phrase *as they went.* God blesses us as we are
doing what we can do.

The earth is filled with minerals to be mined, there are rivers to
be bridged. God gave to us all that we need for a happy, successful, abundant life on this earth, but part of what He gave to us
includes our own abilities, talents, and energies. There are some
things we *must* do for ourselves.

The third finger is *inspiration.*

"Seeing we also are compassed about with so great a cloud of
witnesses, let us lay aside every weight, and the sin which doth so
easily beset us, and let us run with patience the race that is set
before us, Looking unto Jesus the author and finisher of our
faith . . ." (Hebrews 12:1, 2).

Cloud of witnesses—whatever your trouble is, if you look
around you can find others who had the same experiences, and
yet they fought through to victory. There are many who can
testify that circumstances can be overcome. *Looking unto
Jesus*—what an inspiration His life is! He faced sorrows, loneliness, defeat, betrayal, pain, and even death, but He never
did give up and quit. There is inspiration by "looking unto
Jesus."

The fourth finger represents *trust.*

Trust that God is good—that there is somebody who is concerned about us and will help us. William Cullen Bryant watched
a duck flying across the sky and wrote his famous poem "To a
Water Fowl":

> He who, from zone to zone
> Guides through the boundless sky thy certain flight,
> In the long way I must tread alone
> Will lead my steps aright.

The fifth finger stands for the *truth of eternity.*

Life is not limited to the short span of years on this earth. We should be firm believers in "one world at a time," giving all we have to the life that we have. Also we keep realizing there is life beyond life.

Trouble May Be a Blessing

Sometimes—perhaps a majority of the time—it seems that God lets the innocent suffer and the guilty go unpunished. Once there was a great earthquake in San Francisco. A newspaper reporter noticed that a liquor distillery was standing unharmed after the earthquake. He wrote these words:

> If, as they say, God spanked this town
> For being overfrisky,
> Why did He burn the churches down
> And spare old Hopalong's whiskey?

We know that God does not protect His saints and bring disaster on the evil ones. Sometimes it seems even that the best people suffer the most. But we make a great mistake when we infer that our suffering is God's punishing us for our sins.

When Beethoven became deaf in the midst of his brilliant career, his first reaction was utter despair. He said, "What a sorrowful life I must now live. How happy I would be if my hearing would be completely restored." Gradually his attitude changed, though. He went on to write some of his most glorious music.

No person is ever defeated until he or she accepts defeat.

Another point to remember is, "Usually there is no gain without pain."

All of us have hurts and disappointments, but all of us have faith and vision. Life depends on what we choose to emphasize. Mark Twain had some dark periods in his life. During these periods he wrote some letters which were discovered after his death. They disclosed bitterness, unhappiness, and despair. It would have been very easy for him to have surrendered to defeat. On the other hand, he had some strong beliefs. He believed in boys and therefore he could write stories about Tom Sawyer and Huckleberry Finn. In his stories he would make goodness triumph over evil. He believed that could happen. He also believed that he had the ability to write, and he disciplined himself to do it. If Mark Twain had only nursed his bitterness, we would never have heard of him and would never have had his matchless stories.

Remember, there are always hands ready to be stretched forth toward us. Robert Louis Stevenson wrote: "It is friends who stand between us and our self-contempt." We need bridges of appreciation over the troubled waters of our lives. We also need to be such bridges over the troubled waters of other people's lives.

Trouble may really be a blessing. I heard this wonderful story that illustrates that good can come out of evil:

A Norwegian fisherman with his two sons went on their daily fishing run. As usual, the mother went down to the wharf to see her family off and to wish them safety and a good catch. By midafternoon the waves were rolling higher than usual. A sharp, brisk wind whipped little spits of salty spray into the faces of the rugged man and his teenage boys. The wind increased; the waves grew like humped, marine giants of a prehistoric day. The storm caused the little boat to toss and pitch as the three rowed desperately to get back to shore. The fierce storm put out the light in the lighthouse on shore, leaving the fishermen dependent upon dark, groping guesswork.

Meanwhile, in the kitchen of their rustic cottage, a fire broke out. Before the wife and mother could put out the fire, it destroyed their every earthly possession, except the clothes on their backs. Finally, the father and sons were able to row the boat safely to shore. Waiting on the beach to tell them the tragic news of the fire was the wife and mother.

"Karl," she tearfully said, "fire has destroyed our house and all our possessions. We have nothing now."

But Karl seemed strangely unmoved by the disconcerting news.

"Didn't you hear me, Karl? Our house is gone."

"Yes, I heard you," he replied, "but a few hours ago we were lost at sea, riding high waves and death seemed mighty close. Our only guide to the shoreline, the light in the house on the cliff, went out. For an hour I thought death would be our lot. Then something happened: a dim, yellow glow appeared in the distance. Then it grew bigger and bigger. We turned our boat and rowed with all our might to get in the path of that light. When we did, we followed it safely to the shore. You see, Ingrid," he explained, "that little yellow glow was the first sight of our house burning. At the peak of the blaze, we could see that shoreline as bright as day. The same heat that destroyed our house created a light which saved our lives."

Broken—But Mended Again

Earlier in this chapter we reminded ourselves of the ten lepers who were healed. There is another point that we need to remember just now. That is: "One of them, when he saw that he was healed, turned back, and with a loud voice glorified God" (Luke 17:15). Then to this man Jesus said, ". . . thy faith hath made thee whole" (v. 19). We could spend a good deal of time wondering why the other nine did not come back to thank the Lord. Perhaps they were bitter about the losses of their businesses while they were sick.

Maybe they were anxious to see their families and friends. Maybe they had other reasons, but in coming back to express gratitude, this one man received not only "healing," but "wholeness." He became a complete person. There are many people who have been healed, but they really never overcame their troubles. Some of the most incomplete people are seemingly trouble-free people. Being delivered from trouble is one blessing. Expressing gratitude for the goodness that has come our way is a much greater blessing.

Remember that troubles not only have the power to make us, they also measure us. There is a book *An Episode of Sparrows* by Rumer Godden. In it we read, "You are making a mountain out of a molehill," said Angela.

Olivia was suddenly inspired to answer, "A molehill can be a mountain to a sparrow."

Don't give your life to trying to explain everything that happened. You just cannot understand all of the ways of life. After the loss of his children, his wealth, and his health, JB exclaims:

> "Knew . . . if I knew why! . . .
> What I *can't* bear is the blindness—
> Meaninglessness—the numb blow
> Fallen in the stumbling night."
> ARCHIBALD MACLEISH

There is another quotation to remember, "The tragedy is not that things are broken. The tragedy is that they are not mended again" (Alan Paton, *Cry, The Beloved Country*).

We should not take a Pollyanna attitude towards suffering. Sometimes it is hard and almost unbearable. Not long ago I visited a man whose thirteen-year-old son was suddenly killed. Without really thinking, I said to him, "If I were in your place, I just do not believe I could stand this." He turned to me and said, "That's the most comforting thing you could have said to me."

Sometimes we need to admit that we are not made of iron, that we do have feelings and weaknesses and that we can be hurt. But, praise God, we also admit that we have strengths and powers and that life can go on. We sometimes think that we just cannot stand this which has happened, but we can stand it, and we do stand it by the grace of God. When trouble comes you may *live* alone, but you are *not* alone.

Let's remember the words of one who said: "I am an old man and have had many troubles, but most of them have never happened."

> Some of your hurts you have cured,
> And the sharpest you still have survived,
> But what torments of grief you endured
> From evils that never arrived!
>
> RALPH WALDO EMERSON,
"Borrowing"

So, whether trouble is real or unreal, it isn't the end of living.

9

You Can Believe Your Future In

There are many people living alone with a gloomy outlook of hopeless despair. They have real difficulty in believing that anything good can ever happen in their lives.

I have a minister friend, Dr. Hoover Ruppert, who tells this story: A kind minister became concerned about a poor-looking man he frequently saw sitting in front of the cigar store. One day the minister put two dollars into this man's hand and whispered to him the words, "Never despair."

The next day the man stopped the minister and handed him sixteen dollars.

"What is the meaning of this?" the minister asked.

The man replied, "It means that Never Despair won the fourth race at the Santa Anita track and paid eight to one."

That is not the greatest story in the world but it does have a point. "Never despair" may pay off more than you think.

Here are two sentences consisting of exactly the same words, and at first they seem to mean the same thing; yet they are very different: (1) "I believe in the future." (2) "I believe the future in." Study those two sentences. The second sentence is saying that if you believe, you can create a future. There is marvelous power when you start believing. Too many people have surrendered to despair—even these famous ones:

In 1801 William Wilberforce said, "I dare not marry, the future is too uncertain."

In 1806 William Pitt said, "There is scarcely anything around us but ruin and despair."

In 1848 Lord Shaftesbury said, "Nothing can save the British Empire from shipwreck."

In 1849 Disraeli said, "In industry, commerce, and agriculture there is no hope."

In 1852 the dying Duke of Wellington said, "I thank God I shall be spared from seeing the consummation of ruin that is gathering about us."

Those quotations were taken from the years 1801–1852, yet during that same period of years the following babies were born: Abraham Lincoln, Charles Darwin, Felix Mendelssohn, William E. Gladstone, Cyrus McCormick, Alfred Lord Tennyson, Edgar Allan Poe, and Oliver Wendell Holmes. These men made tremendous accomplishments in the areas of science, industry, government, agriculture, and literature. We have every reason to believe that during the period in which we are now living, babies are being born who in years to come will also make magnificent contributions to the life of this world.

When it comes to our own particular lives, let me emphasize the fact that "you can believe the future in." If you just start believing, you are going to create a future for yourself.

Many of us who are living alone would do well to read the words of the songs that Oscar Hammerstein wrote. He once said, "I just can't write anything without hope in it." Here are some of the words written by him that are familiar to most of us:

> Oh, what a beautiful morning,
> Oh, what a beautiful day!
> I've got a glorious feeling
> Everything's going my way.
> From *Oklahoma!*

In the show *South Pacific* one of the songs contains these words:

> I'm stuck like a dope
> With a thing called hope,
> And I can't get it out of my heart.

In his beautiful musical *The Sound of Music* he wrote:

> Climb every mountain,
> Search high and low,
> Follow every by-way,
> Every path you know.
> Climb every mountain,
> Ford every stream,
> Follow every rainbow,
> 'Til you find your dream.

In "believing your future in" we need to learn to live with some things that cannot be changed. One of the unchangeable things of our lives is our own past. If happy memories come out of your past, it is not hard to live with those. But it is hard to live with some of the sad memories that bring regret and sorrow. Sometimes memories of the past can destroy both our desire to live in the present or in the future. At some time or other, every one of us has said words to this effect: "If only I could have my time to live over again! If only I had done differently in the past!" The truth is, we just need to accept the fact that the past is a part of us. We cannot deny it, or excuse it, or get rid of it.

Concentrate on this glorious thought: *You can believe your future in.* That means that you can make a new past for yourself. Some would call it a "new life." Others might call it "being born again." But, it is glorious to realize that there will come a day when we can look back on the next years—I emphasize *next* years—and they will be a new past for us. The point is, we have a past, but, we also can create another past. So, let us stop looking back and let us begin believing our future in.

I like this:

"THE BEST IS YET TO COME"

Was it so long ago?—seems like yesterday
I was chasing rainbows and playing in the hay.
Was it so long ago? I played hookey from school,
Reading, writing, 'rithmetic, and learning the golden rule?
I remember the school marm saying, "The best is yet to come."
Finally I settled down with a mate for life—
Gosh, was it so long ago we were new as man and wife?
Children they came, our pride and joys . . . Oh yes, the tears
And heartaches with our girls and boys.
They flew the coop one by one. Was it so long ago raising our
Children all done? Oh, I know, "The best is yet to come."
The house sure is quiet now, and we have each other, but
Every now and then I think I hear "Father? . . . Mother?"
Was it so long ago, my mate was taken away? Oh, yes, I know
    what
They say: "The best is yet to come."
My hearing is not so good and I now use a cane . . . .
Was it so long ago I danced in the rain?
Well, Lord, I've been so richly blessed, a wonderful mate,
Beautiful children, and, yes . . . a few regrets . . .
For you see I know at the last setting sun . . .
    "The best is yet to come."

RITA JEAN UNDERWOOD

The Game Is Not Yet Over

One of the greatest temptations in life is to give up too soon. Many of us watch baseball games on television and many times we hear the announcer say, "The game is never over until the last man is out." Time and time again, a team has come into the ninth inning, appearing to be hopelessly defeated, and then scores enough runs to win the game. There are an astonishing number of people who are convinced that the game is over and that they are defeated. Somebody needs to remind them that the game is *not* over.

Doctor Clarence J. Forsberg preached a sermon entitled "Broken Plays and Long Gainers." From his sermon I want to quote these paragraphs:

Some years ago Theodore Parker Ferris told about two individuals with whom he had visited on the same day. He had boarded a train in the evening and no sooner settled himself in a club-car chair than he was approached by a well-dressed, obviously affluent stranger. Dr. Ferris was wearing a clerical collar, and it served as an invitation for the man to unburden himself. The man had been drinking, Ferris said. He was drinking, it turned out, to blunt the pain of a severe personal tragedy. His wife and two children had been killed in a plane crash. It made no sense to him at all. He had decided that God was some kind of heartless monster to let such a thing happen. It was all God's fault. Now there was nothing left to live for.

When at last Ferris was able to excuse himself and retire to the privacy of his compartment, he reflected on the man's misfortune and how he was responding to it. And he thought about Father Daniel S. Lord, the Catholic priest and writer, with whom he had shared the platform that day at an interfaith clergy conference. Father Lord had learned some time earlier that he had cancer. He was sixty-six years old, and the cancer was in both lungs. It was too far gone for surgery. But life was not over. This is what Father Lord had written about his own situation:

"When I first got word of incurable cancer, I must admit that I got the feeling of relief. Some diseases I wouldn't have the patience to bear, but cancer is not one of them. By learning the true facts early, I have been given an opportunity to clean up a lot of unfinished work and to see friends I have been neglecting. Then too I find that life has become very precious. The world looks good to me, and time has become so valuable that I try to squeeze every second that I can from every hour. I have become even more acutely aware of everything around me. If, for me, the end of life were really the end of the road, I suppose I would dread it. But I don't believe it is. I think it is only the beginning of a more abundant life."

At this point many of us would be reminded of one of the real peaks in all of literature—Stephen Benet's *John Brown's Body*. Many of us have read these words again and again. We find in them inspiration and the courage to keep going. If one studies these words they become strength for our souls and inspiration for our lives. They are about a man who was in darkness in our world. Abraham Lincoln is speaking in contest with God. Benet puts these words in Lincoln's mouth:

I've never found a church that I could join
Although I've prayed in churches in my time . . . .
And now I pray to You and You alone.
Teach me to know Your will. Teach me to read
Your difficult purpose here, which must be plain
If I had eyes to see it. Make me just.

There was a man I knew near Pigeon Creek
Who kept a kennel full of hunting dogs,
Young dogs and old, smart hounds and silly hounds.
He'd sell the young ones every now and then,
Smart as they were and slick as they could run.
But the one dog he'd never sell or lend
Was an old half-deaf foolish-looking hound
You wouldn't think had sense to scratch a flea

Unless the flea were old and sickly too.
Most days he used to lie beside the stove
Or sleeping in a piece of sun outside.
Folks used to plague the man about that dog
And he'd agree to everything they said,
"No—he ain't much on looks—or much on speed—
A young dog can outrun him any time,
Outlook him and outeat him and outleap him,
But, Mister, that dog's hell on a cold scent
And, once he gets his teeth in what he's after,
He don't let go until he knows he's dead."

I am that old, deaf hunting-dog, Lord,
And the world's kennel holds ten thousand hounds
Smarter and faster and with finer coats
To hunt Your hidden purpose up the wind
And bell upon the trace You leave behind.
But, when even they fail and lose the scent,
I will keep on because I must keep on
Until You utterly reveal Yourself
And sink my teeth in justice soon or late.
There is no more to ask of earth or fire
And water only runs between my hands,
But in the air, I'll look, in the blue air,
The old dog, muzzle down to the cold scent,
Day after day, until the tired years
Crackle beneath his feet like broken sticks
And the last barren bush consumes with peace . . . .

Therefore I utterly lift up my hands
To You, and here and now beseech Your aid.
I have held back when others tugged me on,
I have gone on when others pulled me back
Striving to read Your will, striving to find
The justice and expedience of this case,

Hunting an arrow down the chilly airs
Until my eyes are blind with the great wind
And my heart sick with running after peace.
And now, I stand and tremble on the last
Edge of the last blue cliff, a hound beat out,
Tail down and belly flattened to the ground,
My lungs are breathless and my legs are whipped,
Everything in me's whipped except my will.
I can't go on, And yet, I must go on.

What Men Live By

Doctor Richard C. Cabot was chief of the medical staff of Massachusetts General Hospital. Not only was he a great physician, he was also a great person. He wrote about a dozen books which have inspired many people. Perhaps the book he wrote that is the best known and best loved is *What Men Live By*. In it he points out that there are four important facets to every well-balanced life—work, play, love, worship. One of the surest ways to begin "believing your future in" is to begin living today. We cannot find a better formula than the one Dr. Cabot gave us.

WORK.   Let us look at his first suggestion. Uselessness is probably the most destructive state in which a person can live. All of us have dreamed of the time when we could do as we please and not be compelled to work at anything. When such thoughts come into my mind, I remind myself of the story of the little boy who had been playing outside. He came into the house and was getting in his mother's way. She suggested to him that he go back out into the yard.

He asked, "What can I do?"

She replied, "Do whatever you want to do."

He answered, "Mama, I am *tired* of doing what I want to do."

There is a lot of food for thought in that little story. We need obligations in life. We need burdens to bear, dreams to dream,

work to accomplish. Badger Clark wrote this poem—"The Job."
He comes nearer expressing the importance of work and its
meaning than anything I have ever read. Every so often I read
this with appreciation and inspiration.

THE JOB

But, God, it won't come right! It won't come right!
I've worked it over till my brain is numb.
The first flash came so bright,
Then more ideas after it—flash! flash!
I thought it some new constellation men would wonder at!
Perhaps it's just a fire-work—flash! fizz! spat!
Then darker darkness and scorched pasteboard and sour smoke;
But, God, the thought was great,
The Scheme, the dream—why, till the first charm broke
The thing just built itself while I, elate,
Laughed and admired it. Then it stuck,
Half done, the lesser half, worse luck!
You see, it's dead as yet, a frame, a body—and the heart,
The soul, the fiery, vital part
To give it life, is what I cannot get. I've tried—
You know it—tried to catch live fire,
And pawed cold ashes. Every spark has died.
It won't come right! I'd drop the thing entire,
Only, I can't! I love my job.

You who ride the thunder,
Do You know what it is to dream and drudge and throb? I
        wonder—
Did it come to You with a rush, Your dream, Your plan?
If so, I know how You began.
Yes, with rapt face and sparkling eyes,
Swinging the hot globe out between the skies,
Marking the new seas with their white beach lines,
Sketching in sun, and moon, the lightning and the rains,

Sowing the hills with pines,
Wreathing a rim of purple round the plains,
I know You laughed then, while You caught and wrought
The big, swift, rapturous outline of Your thought. And then,
    MAN!

I see it now,
O God, forget my pettish row!
I see Your job! While ages crawl
Your lips take laboring lines, Your eyes a sadder light,
For man, the fire and flower and center of it all—
Man can't come right!
After Your patient centuries,
Fresh starts, recasting, tired Gethsemanes
And tense Golgothas, he, Your central theme
Is just a jangling echo of Your dream.
Grand as the rest may be, he ruins it.
Why don't You quit?
Crumple it all and dream again?
But, no;
Flaw after flaw, You work it out, revise, refine—
Bondage, brutality, and war and woe,
The sot, the fool, the tyrant, and the mob—
Dear God, how You must love Your job!
Help me, as I love mine.

                                        BADGER CLARK

PLAY.   Work alone is not sufficient. The second part of life
which is of vital importance, according to Dr. Cabot, is *play*.

We are familiar with the old proverb: "All work and no play
makes Jack a dull boy." Play includes rest, relaxation, and a
change of activity. Without play one becomes tense, grim, and
self-centered. One-fourth of life should be given to play. We need
to remember that the word recreation really means re-creation.
We need to learn to forget ourselves in some activity that we

really enjoy. It is a pitiful person who has forgotten the meaning of fun.

One of the great statesmen of all time was Sir Winston Churchill. He had several recreational activities. One of them was bricklaying. He enjoyed building with bricks. Another one of his recreations was painting lovely landscapes.

Many people are familiar with the popular folksinger, Mac Davis. One of the songs that he made famous goes like this:

> You got to stop and smell the roses,
> You got to count your many blessings
> Every day—
> You gonna find the way to Heaven is
> A rough and rocky road
> If you don't stop and smell the roses
> Along the way.*

That song reminds us of Jesus' saying to people, ". . . Consider the lilies of the field, how they grow . . ." (Matthew 6:28). We can let worries and anxieties become heavy burdens. We can remember the guilts of yesterday and the fears of the tomorrows. But, Jesus pointed out that the wild flowers of the earth do not worry. They accept the tender care of God and they are beautiful creations.

Tennyson expressed the same thought in these beloved words:

> Flower in the crannied wall,
> I pluck you out of the crannies,
> I hold you here, root and all, in my hand,
> Little flower—but *if* I could understand
> What you are, root and all, and all in all,
> I should know what God and man is.

The problem is, we get so busy with the work of life that we forget about the flowers and the beauty of life.

We have read part of Mac Davis's "You Got to Stop and Smell the Roses." Another part goes like this:

Hey, mister, where you goin' in such a hurry?
Don't you think it's time you realize
There's a whole lot more to life than work and worry—
The sweetest things in life are free,
And they're right before your eyes.

You gonna find the way to Heaven is
A rough and rocky road
If you don't stop and smell the roses
Along the way.

Sometimes in the work of making a living, we forget to make a life.

Play is one of the things that Dr. Cabot tells us that we must live by. Or, as Mac Davis put it, "You got to stop and smell the roses."

LOVE.   Love is the third principle which Dr. Cabot says is *What Men Live By*.

Love Against Hate is the title of a book written by the famed psychiatrist Dr. Karl Menninger. In it he reminds us that there are many ways of dealing with our resentment, frustration, hostility, and the resulting violence and destruction. He makes it very clear that work can heal many wounds. Work can change our anger and frustration, it can restore us to physical health. Creative work is one of the essentials of life.

Equally important are *play, recreation,* and *relaxation*. Doctor Menninger himself, was an expert at the game of chess. A person who has no joyful outlets of recreation is really potentially dangerous.

Ultimately, however, human survival on this earth depends upon *genuine love*. Love gives one the strength to cope with the hardships of human existence, while hate defeats a person even before the struggle begins. Love gives one a purpose for being here. Let us read a quotation from *The Magnificent Defeat* by Frederick Buechner:

The love for equals is a human thing . . . of friend for friend,
brother for brother. It is to love what is loving and lovely.
The world smiles.
The love for the less fortunate is a beautiful thing . . . the love for
those who suffer, for those who are poor, the sick, the failures,
the unlovely. This is compassion, and it touches the
heart of the world.
The love for the more fortunate is a rare thing . . . to love those
who succeed where we fail, to rejoice without envy with
those who rejoice, the love of the poor for the rich, of the
black man for the white man. The world is bewildered
by its saints.
And then there is the love for the enemy . . . love for the one
who does not love you but mocks, threatens, and inflicts
pain. The tortured's love for the torturer.
THIS IS GOD'S LOVE. IT CONQUERS THE WORLD.

Why Do We Love?

We must remember that God gave us power to hate, and hate
is not always a bad thing. It depends on what we hate, and there
are a lot of things that need hating, such as, war, racism, slums,
prostitution, mistreatment of children, and many other conditions.

The problem, however, is to hate and at the same time to love;
to be angry but at the same time to be fair and just; to oppose
wrongs and at the same time preserve the Christian spirit. There
are times when hatred is not only permissible but obligatory.

The problem is how to hate and love at the same time: the best
approach I know is to hate things and not persons. We blame
individuals and persuade ourselves that their punishment will
make everything all right. Such is never the case. We need impersonal hatred of evil. We can be *too* conformist, too submis-
sive, too timid. We can make no protest when decency is ignored. Sometimes the silence of good people is appalling. We
should not stop our denunciation of evil; neither must we stop
our expressions of love.

A good question for us to ask is, "Why do we love others?" When it comes to certain people, such as our family circle, the answer is obvious. As we go along through life and make friends, we can understand that love. It is also natural to love those who are very lovable. We love little children and we love people who are in need.

But, why would one be a Good Samaritan, stopping on the highway to help an injured person who is a complete stranger? That is not an easy question to answer. Some may stop and help because it is the decent thing to do. Others may stop because their religion requires it. Such reasons as these are self-interest.

The true spirit of the Good Samaritan goes beyond mere human interest and emotion. Our caring for people, whether they are friends or strangers, pretty or ugly, good or bad, comes from a Divine Source. We recall that Jesus said, "Thou shalt love the Lord thy God with all thy heart, and with all thy soul, and with all thy mind. This is the first and great commandment. And the second is like unto it. Thou shalt love thy neighbour as thyself. On these two commandments hang all the law and the prophets" (Matthew 22:37–40). Here we see it made very clear that we cannot love other people until first we love God. We learn to love people by first loving God.

How Do We Love?

Not only are we concerned with *why* we love; another question is "How do we love?" We can talk about the suffering world, but we cannot lead where we are not going.

This should make us both care and share.

I was hungry
    and you formed a humanities club
    and you discussed my hunger.
    Thank you.

I was imprisoned
  and you crept off quietly
  to your chapel in the cellar
  and prayed for my release.

I was naked
  and in your mind
  you debated the morality of my
  appearance.

I was sick
  and you knelt and thanked God
  for your health.

I was homeless
  and you preached to me
  of the spiritual shelter of the
  love of God.

I was lonely
  and you left me alone
  to pray for me.

You seem so holy;
  so close to God.
  But I'm still very hungry
  and lonely
    and cold.

So where have your prayers gone?
  What have they done?
  What does it profit a man to page through his book of prayers
    when the rest of the world is crying for help?

                                    The Churchman
                                    Diocese of Dallas

For some years Dr. Clarence J. Forsberg has been kind enough to share his sermons in mimeograph form. I have been fortunate to be on his mailing list and have regularly read his penetrating insight. Here is one of his splendid communion meditations:

A MONUMENT TO SPIRIT

One of the traits or characteristics of human personality, which has been evident down through the centuries, is the desire on the part of man to be remembered. Most of us like to be recognized while we're still alive, and I suspect that all of us would like to be remembered after we are gone. Men have done strange things in order to perpetuate their names after death. They have built monuments, some of which are beautiful and some of which are grotesque. They have gone to extreme measures in order to insure a kind of immortality on earth.

A few years ago someone sent me a newspaper story about one such monument which is not too far from Lincoln, Kansas. It was built by a man named John Davis, who lived and died near Hiawatha, Kansas. He was a farmer, and he was a self-made man. He started out as a hired hand, and by determination and frugality he managed to amass a considerable fortune in his lifetime. He did not, incidentally, make many friends. When he was married some fifty years ago, his wife's family thought that she had married beneath her. He reciprocated their dislike. He and his wife had no children, and he was determined not to leave any money to his in-laws.

When she died, he decided that he wanted to erect a statue in memory of her. He had an artist design a statue which showed both her and him at opposite ends of a love seat. He liked it so much that he commissioned another statue, this time of himself, kneeling at his wife's grave, and placing a wreath on it. That impressed him enough so that he commissioned still another statue, this time of his wife, kneeling at his future grave site, depositing a wreath. (Since she was no longer alive, he had the sculptor add a pair of wings to make an angel out of her.) One thing led to another until he had spent some two hundred and fifty thousand dollars on the monument to his wife and himself.

On occasion, someone from the town would suggest that

he might be interested in doing something with his money
for others. There was a project to build a hospital, and
another to build a swimming pool for the kids. He turned a
deaf ear on all such pleas. "What has the town ever done for
me?" he asked. "I don't owe this town nothin'."

He spent all his money on those statues, and eventually
he had used up his resources. He died at the age of ninety-
two, a resident in the poorhouse. Very few people attended
the final rites for Mr. Davis, and it is reported that only one
person seemed genuinely moved by any sense of personal
loss. It was Horace England, who was the tombstone sales-
man.

The strange thing about this monument is that it is slowly
sinking into the ground. Davis left no money to maintain it.
The townspeople show no particular concern in perpetuat-
ing it. Eventually it will be gone, a victim of time, vandalism,
and neglect.

Now, why do I tell you this story about the man who spent
all his money on a monument so that none of it would go to
his wife's relatives? I do it because it represents a monument
to spite. He loved no one except himself and his wife. He
gave no one any reason to love him. He built a monument
that would outlast him by a few years, but in the end it turns
out to be a sad reminder of an unsympathetic, self-centered,
eccentric life. There is a certain poetic justice in the fact that
within a few years, it will all be gone.

Two thousand years ago a man lived who did not amass a
fortune. He spent Himself in the service of others. He was
like all men in the sense that He wanted to be remembered.
On the night before He died He gathered His friends around
a table in an upper room, and gave them the simplest kind of
memorial that you could imagine. He broke bread and gave
it to them, and said, "Take, eat; this is my body broken for
you." Then He took the chalice, and said, "Drink ye all of it;
this is my blood which is shed for you. As oft as ye do this,
do it in remembrance of me."

Two thousand years have passed since that night, and that monument remains. It shines brighter today than ever before. It is a dramatic reminder that the only thing that lasts in this world is love. "Now abideth faith, hope, and love; and the greatest of these is love."

What Love Is Not

We have been talking about love. Perhaps it is time we say a few things about what love is *not*.

For example, recognition is not love. It is important to recognize a person as a person and to recognize a person's accomplishment and place in society. Being ignored or overlooked is a difficult experience to bear. Yet recognizing is not the same as loving.

There are some people who feel that it is better to be treated badly than to be ignored. Across the years, I have talked with both wives and husbands who were abused by the other. They did not get a divorce because at least they were being recognized by the other—but they were not being loved.

On the other hand, positive attention may not be love. A husband may phone his wife five times a day from the office. He may bring flowers and candy and gifts. He may give her all manner of attention, but still not be in love with her. And, vice versa, the wife may prepare just the meals that he wants, keep his clothes in proper care and order, constantly compliment him and do all the things that he wants—and still not love him.

I heard a father say to a son sometime ago, "When you consider all that I have given to you in the last three years, how could you doubt that I love you?" This father is making a very great mistake. There is a vast difference in giving and loving. One can give to satisfy his or her own ego, to salve a guilty conscience, or even as a substitute for love.

Neither is love looking up to a person adoringly. We all like to be admired. When someone gives us special attention, it is easy to respond happily and enthusiastically. But being admired is not being loved.

We hear the expression "Love at first sight." I have always thought that was a contradiction in terms. Love is a growing, developing experience. Sexual desire can come at first sight. Infatuation can be a first-sight experience, but, love is a long-range relationship.

Not even sharing is love. Love may involve sharing but not necessarily so. Two people can hope, dream, aspire, and work together without loving each other.

Love includes, to some degree, all of the above, but love goes beyond all of the above. If one really wants to know what love is, then I suggest the reading of the Thirteenth Chapter of 1 Corinthians. That is the best definition that I know. In the church where I am the pastor, not too long ago, I located that chapter in thirty-one different translations, printed them in a pamphlet, and mailed one out to every family in the congregation. I asked each family to read one of the translations each day during the month. During that month, I preached each Sunday a sermon on *Love.* Later the thirty-one translations and the sermons I gave were published in a book entitled *The Miracle of Love.* That book is still enjoying a large sale in the bookstores.

Kahlil Gibran has written about love beautifully.

When love beckons to you, follow him,
Though his ways are hard and steep.
And when his wings enfold you yield to him,
Though the sword hidden among his pinions may wound you.
And when he speaks to you believe in him,
Though his voice may shatter your dreams as the north wind
    lays waste the garden.

For even as love crowns you so shall he crucify you. Even as
    he is for your growth so is he for your pruning . . . .

Like sheaves of corn he gathers you unto himself.
He threshes you to make you naked.

He sifts you to free you from your husks.
He grinds you to whiteness.
He kneads you until you are pliant;
And then he assigns you to his sacred fire, that you may become sacred bread for God's sacred feast . . . .

But if in your fear you would seek only love's peace and love's pleasure,
Then it is better for you that you cover your nakedness and pass out of love's threshing-floor,
Into the seasonless world where you shall laugh, but not all of your laughter, and weep, but not all of your tears . . . .

When you love you should not say, "God is in my heart," but rather, "I am in the heart of God."

God is love . . . God loves you . . . and I love you!

Love Yourself

Don't forget also to love yourself. That means that you are eager to keep yourself worthy of your own self-respect. An old minister used to pray, "Oh, Lord, give me a high opinion of myself." To love yourself is to recognize that you have a mind which is an instrument of God. It means that you believe your body is literally the temple of the Spirit of God and thus must not be desecrated. To love yourself means that you see yourself as an immortal soul who will live throughout eternity.

In loving ourselves, we are not being selfish. The selfish person is only interested in himself or herself and finds little pleasure in giving and great pleasure in taking. The selfish person looks at the world only from the standpoint of what he or she can get out of it, judging everything in terms of its usefulness to him or he Selfishness is really the opposite of self-love. In fact, the selfish person is not even capable of loving himself or herself. Some body once wrote a story in which the main character had no name. That is really the result of selfishness. It leads one to become a nobody.

On the other hand, self-love makes one know that he or she is somebody. You are a person in your own right. To love yourself is to accept yourself as God accepts you. As you discover your own worth, you really begin to discover life. Thus it was that Dr. Cabot listed love as one of the things that men live by.

WORSHIP.   Finally, Dr. Cabot says that men live by *worship.* In *What Men Live By* in *This I Believe,* he says, "Worship renews the spirit as sleep renews the body."

Helen Hayes, the queen of the American theatre, told of an experience that she had in a church when she was facing her greatest sorrow. Her daughter was ill and was slowly reaching the fatal stage. Only a mother could understand the ordeal that Helen Hayes was experiencing. She was driven almost to distraction and went to a church to pray. She looked around and saw a number of people upon whose faces were trouble and sorrow. She realized that life had not been kind to many of them and that they were there in God's House seeking renewal. Then she wrote: "It seemed, as they prayed, that their worn faces lighted up and they became very vessels of God. In my need, I gained strength from the knowledge that they too had needs . . . . I experienced a flood of compassion for people."

She beautifully summed up the meaning of worship in those words: *I gained strength. I experienced a flood of compassion for people.*

Many people believe that the finest account of an experience of worship is recorded in Isaiah 6:1–8. That is truly a tremendous and striking experience.

It begins with: "In the year that King Uzziah died . . ." Isaiah was a young man, King Uzziah was his hero. This was a tremendous shock to his life. Oftentimes our clearest and most vivid experiences of God come out of some deep sorrow. Sorrows have the power to make people either bitter or better. Some people resent and reject God in their sorrows. Others open their hearts to God.

In time of sorrow Isaiah went to the Temple. There he saw the

Lord as he had never seen him before. He realized the glorious, majestic presence of the Holy God. In God's presence, he recognized his own weakness and his own need. He said, "Woe is me! for I am undone; because I am a man of unclean lips, and I dwell in the midst of a people of unclean lips."

Next comes to Isaiah a marvelous, cleansing experience. He felt forgiven and renewed. It was then that he saw a need for service and the climax of his experience of worship is "Here am I; send me."

Both Isaiah and Helen Hayes, in a time of great need, found that people do live by worship.

Practical Atheists

Today we are living in a society that is growing more and more secular. It is a great tragedy. Various polls of the American people have shown that perhaps 95 percent, or more, say that they believe in God. The truth is, great numbers of people do not believe God makes any difference. Many of them are what I call "practical atheists." They admit that a God exists and that perhaps He even created the earth. They do not believe that He has anything to do with the world today or with their own lives.

Religious faith for many people is a very shallow experience. Two men were seated side by side on an airplane. One of them happened to be a great leader in the church, the other one was an internationally known astronomer. As they chatted, the subject of religion came up. The astronomer said to the churchman, "My religion can be summed up in one sentence." Naturally the churchman was very interested in what that sentence might be, so he asked him for it.

The astronomer said, "Do unto others as you would have them do unto you."

The churchman was silent for a moment. Then he said to the astronomer that he could sum up all the science of astronomy in one sentence. Naturally the astronomer was interested and inquired as to what that sentence was.

The churchman replied, "Twinkle, twinkle, little star, how I wonder what you are."

Of course, each of them recognized the superficiality of the other.

Prayer

Real worship is communion and fellowship with God. On one occasion one of the disciples said to Jesus, "Lord, teach us to pray . . ." (Luke 11:1). This is the only thing they ever asked Jesus to teach them. The disciples never asked Jesus to teach them to preach, to heal, to perform miracles, how to organize churches, or even how to win the world. They realized that the essence of worship—the essence of faith—the essence of life—is prayer. When we learn to pray, all of the other relationships with God will come. There are five essential facts that we need to know about prayer. Let me state them briefly:

First, prayer is "the soul's sincere desire, unuttered or expressed." That is, prayer is part of both our consciousness and our unconsciousness.

Second, prayer is being connected with power or energy or force, which is both within people and yet completely surrounds people.

Third, prayer is experiencing fellowship with an ever-present God.

Fourth, prayer is all of life. It is every thought, every feeling, every act.

Fifth, prayer is seeking to understand one's own life and one's own self. If through prayer we come to know and experience the God of love, then it becomes truly power in our lives. On the other hand, if we think of God as a God of punishment, retaliation and one to be feared, then prayer develops within us a feeling of insecurity and lack of worth.

The Lord's Prayer

If one would learn to pray, begin with the Lord's Prayer, which is recorded in Matthew 6:9–13.

It begins, *Our Father.* We begin by thinking about God. Someone has asked why we close our eyes when we pray. Perhaps the reason is so that we may shut out the world in order to give our complete attention to God. However, true prayer opens our eyes so that we may see God. There is a hymn that beautifully expresses it:

> Open my eyes, that I may see
> Glimpses of truth Thou hast for me.
> CLARA H. SCOTT

As we pray, we want God's name to be "hallowed"— revered—revealed.

Thy kingdom come.

It is much easier to pray *Thy kingdom go.* It is easier to pray for somebody else than honestly to face our own lives. The kingdom must "come" before we can make it "go."

Thy will be done.

We frequently express our opinions as to what ought to happen in our world. In true prayer we are more concerned about what God wants to happen.

Give us this day our daily bread.

We are not self-sufficient. We are dependent. All people stand equally before God in their need.

Forgive us . . . as we forgive others.

Guilt can be taken away and the hot fires of resentment within our own hearts can be quenched.

Lead us not into temptation.

Many people go through life dreading some tragedy that might happen. When it comes, they find that they have strengths that they did not realize they had. On the other hand, many go through life believing they are strong enough to withstand any temptation. When the temptation comes, they find weaknesses that they did not know they had.

Thine is the kingdom . . . .

The end and climax of all worship is the glorification of God. If God be glorified, then we are most blessed.

Prayer Result

Prayer is really the same as the dominant desire of the human soul. We are responsible for our own prayer lives. We cannot put that responsibility on any other person. Through the years I have never known a person to become healed who has continued to blame mother and father, brother or sister, or anybody else— even God—for what has happened to his or her life. True prayer puts the person in his or her own true light. The very essence of prayer therapy is that we are made in the image of God. Get the right image of God and the right self-image will come to you.

The result of true prayer is that instead of lameness, people walk; instead of hating, they love; instead of being critical, they congratulate; instead of being spiteful, they serve; instead of being resentful, they accept it.

Worship

Consecration—meditation—contemplation—adoration—inter-cession—supplication—thanksgiving—silence. All of these are a part of worship.

What *do* men live by? The answer is—*work, play, love* and *worship.*

**The following two affirmations help me
as I work toward believing my own future in.**

I DO NOT KNOW WHAT THE FUTURE HOLDS
OF JOY OR PAIN,
OF LOSS OR GAIN,
ALONG LIFE'S UNTROD WAY;
BUT I BELIEVE
I CAN RECEIVE
GOD'S PROMISED GUIDANCE DAY BY DAY;
SO I SECURELY TRAVEL ON.

AND IF, AT TIMES, THE JOURNEY LEADS
THROUGH WATERS DEEP,
OR MOUNTAINS STEEP,
I KNOW THIS UNSEEN FRIEND,
HIS LOVE REVEALING,
HIS PRESENCE HEALING,
WALKS WITH ME TO THE JOURNEY'S END;
SO I SECURELY TRAVEL ON.

AUTHOR UNKNOWN

And I said to the man who stood at the gate of the year: Give me a Light that I may tread safely into the unknown!

And he replied: Go out into the darkness and put thine hand into the hand of God. That shall be to thee better than light and safer than a known way.